Return to Innocence

Return to Innocence

Cultivating Passion *for* Purity

Mark Richardson

© 2004 by Dr. Mark Richardson. All rights reserved.

Printed in the United States of America

Packaged by Pleasant Word, a division of WinePress Publishing, PO Box 428, Enumclaw, WA 98022. The views expressed or implied in this work do not necessarily reflect those of Pleasant Word, a division of WinePress Publishing. Ultimate design, content, and editorial accuracy of this work are the responsibilities of the author.

No part of this publication may be reproduced, stored in a retrieval system, or transmitted in any way by any means—electronic, mechanical, photocopy, recording, or otherwise—without the prior permission of the copyright holder, except as provided by USA copyright law.

Unless otherwise noted, all Scriptures are taken from the Holy Bible, New International Version, Copyright © 1973, 1978, 1984 by the International Bible Society. Used by permission of Zondervan Publishing House. The "NIV" and "New International Version" trademarks are registered in the United States Patent and Trademark Office by International Bible Society.

Scripture references marked RSV are taken from the Revised Standard Version of the Bible, copyright © 1952 [2nd edition, 1971] by the Division of Christian Education of the National Council of the Churches of Christ in the United States of America. Used by permission. All rights reserved.

Scripture references marked NASB are taken from the New American Standard Bible, © 1960, 1963, 1968, 1971, 1972, 1973, 1975, 1977 by The Lockman Foundation. Used by permission.

ISBN 1-4141-0180-5
Library of Congress Catalog Card Number: 2004092534

TABLE OF CONTENTS

Foreword 9
Introduction 13

Committing to Innocence 15
   Day One: Innocence Lost 15
   Day Two: Wise About What Is Good 19
   Day Three: The Value and Importance of Wisdom ... 25
   Day Four: Good 33
   Day Five: Innocent 39
   Day Six: Evil 42

Raising the Standard 47
   Day Seven: Living on a Higher Plane 47
   Day Eight: Focusing on Jesus 50
   Day Nine: Focusing on Heaven 53
   Day Ten: Flesh vs. Spirit 56
   Day Eleven: Renew Your Mind 60
   Day Twelve: Guard Your Eyes and Ears 64
   Day Thirteen: Absolute Surrender 66

Sowing to the Spirit 71
   Day Fourteen: The Role of the Spirit 71
   Day Fifteen: The Fruit of the Spirit Is Love 75
   Day Sixteen: The Fruit of the Spirit Is Joy 80
   Day Seventeen: The Fruit of the Spirit Is Peace 83
   Day Eighteen: The Fruit of the Spirit Is Patience 85
   Day Nineteen: The Fruit of the Spirit Is Kindness 92
   Day Twenty: The Fruit of the Spirit Is Goodness 95
   Day Twenty-one: The Fruit of the Spirit Is Faithfulness 99
   Day Twenty-two: The Fruit of the Spirit Is Gentleness 102
   Day Twenty-three: The Fruit of the Spirit Is Self-Control 106

Getting Practical 111
   Day Twenty-four: Overcoming Compulsive Behavior 111
   Day Twenty-five: The Replacement Principle 115
   Day Twenty-six: Study 120
   Day Twenty-seven: Meditate 124
   Day Twenty-eight: Pray 127
   Day Twenty-nine: Examine Yourself 131
   Day Thirty: Memorize 134
   Day Thirty-one: Spiritual Exercises 136
   Day Thirty-two: Association 143

Putting on Your Armor 147
   Day Thirty-three: The Breastplate of Righteousness 147
   Day Thirty-four: The Belt of Truth 153
   Day Thirty-five: The Gospel of Peace and the Helmet of
      Salvation 157
   Day Thirty-six: The Shield of Faith 165
   Day Thirty-seven: The Sword of the Spirit 169

Victory Is Here 173
   Day Thirty-eight: You Will Never Stumble 173
   Day Thirty-nine: Gaining the Victory 181

Day Forty: Tying It All Together 183
Bibliography 187
Endnotes 197

Foreword

Feeling trapped is frightening, even for the bravest of souls. Nothing tests a soldier's fighting mettle like an ambush. And why did 9/11 knock the wind out of us? People were suddenly trapped and ultimately lost their lives in a place they thought was safe.

These feelings can be understood by more than just soldiers and survivors of war and terror. Anyone who has been snared by sexual temptation (or any repetitive struggle), held hostage by sin's iron grip, and felt as if life was being crushed by its affects knows this terrifying trap all too well.

Is this book for you, or maybe for someone you love? Because you picked it up, the answer is yes. No generation in the history of humanity has bypassed the satanic attack of sexual sin. Yet no generation has been assaulted to the degree as has the present. With the addition of the Internet to the weapons of the media, sexual addictions have crossed the gender boundary in percentages never seen before. Our youth are being snared into sexual addictions quite often before they even enter puberty. And men, many of whom were barely treading water against the undertow of this dangerous river of temptation, are now drowning.

Is this situation hopeless? Are more families, careers, churches, and individuals doomed to destruction because of this raging terror? The answer is no. Can anyone help? The answer is yes. Mark Richardson is a uniquely qualified guide for navigating this treacherous journey. First, Mark is a personal survivor and conqueror in the battle against sexual addiction. His nearly twenty-five years of experience in the addiction and his personal recovery give him eyes to see what is behind and beneath this insidious snare. His training in counseling, doctorate in ministry, work in sexual addiction recovery, and deep walk with the Lord prepared him with the professional and spiritual experience to write on the pages of this book the walk he lives.

I have known Mark for more than a decade and have served side by side with him in ministry now for almost two years. I have been led, taught, and encouraged by Mark's passion for the Lord and his commitment to purity. In this book you can expect these blessings:

1. Mark will guide you through an honest assessment of where you are spiritually.
2. Mark will then help you to understand why the purity you long for is absolutely critical to regain a life that is no longer driven and oppressed by shame.
3. The journey will continue with an in-depth study into Scriptures that pack the power needed to renew our minds to a new way of life.
4. Finally, Mark will give you a model for building a meaningful and practical relationship with Christ and with the Holy Spirit who will give you the guidance and the staying power needed to make this change to purity permanent!

Repetitive sin of any kind can be traced to the same source: a breakdown in our relationship with God. This does not have to be. No matter where you are right now, even if you are completely engulfed in sin,

Foreword

the One who loves you most is ready to give you an immediate and complete fresh start. This book may be the first gift He gives you on the way to the ultimate gift of a new life of purity, self-control, lasting and enjoyable relationships, and ultimately eternal pleasure in heaven. God be with you on this journey, and let it begin right now.

—Don McLaughlin
March 2004

Introduction

> I want you to be wise about what is good, and innocent about what is evil. (Rom. 16:19b)

It would be wonderful if everyone who became a Christian was automatically innocent again. No more lust, no more evil thoughts, no more temptations. But just because a person has been born again does not mean that he will no longer struggle with temptation. The Christian has been washed by the precious blood of Jesus and has been sanctified. But many of the desires, habits and temptations may still be present. Throughout this study we will examine Romans 16:19, which tells God's people to be *wise about what is good* and *innocent about what is evil*. How can we be wise about what is good? What does it mean to be innocent about what is evil? How do we return to innocence when we realize that our innocence has been lost? These are some of the questions we will answer. The primary purpose for this study will be to examine some practical things we can do to return to being innocent about things that are evil and at the same time learn to be wise about what is good.

Please do not just read the words of this book! Take your Bible and a pen and paper and prayerfully apply each new principle to your life.

Throughout this study it is assumed that the reader is already in Christ.

Unless stated otherwise, the New International Version has been used whenever Scriptures are quoted.

In most cases I have referred to people in the masculine gender. This was done for simplicity and no disrespect for the feminine gender was intended.

COMMITTING TO INNOCENCE

DAY ONE

Innocence Lost

Everyone has heard about your obedience, so I am full of joy over you; but I want you to be wise about what is good, and innocent about what is evil. (Rom. 16:19)

Paul was overjoyed because the people in Rome were walking in obedience to God. But he wanted to end his letter to them with some practical advice that they could use to help them grow. So he gave them a couple of areas to work on. First, learn to be wise about what is good. Second, learn to be innocent about what is evil.

Before we came to Christ we were all living in darkness (1 Pet. 2:9) and were following the ways of the world (Eph 2:1–3). Each one of us had struggles and temptations. Regardless of how young or old a person was when he made the decision to obey the gospel, he came to Christ with all of his experiences and his environment helping to develop who he was the day he first believed. Let's begin by examining the struggles and temptations that many of the young people in the world face each day. We can easily see how these things can have an impact on people's lives and on the choices they make. Every day in America the following statements are true:

1,000 unwed teenage girls become mothers
1,106 teenage girls get abortions
4,219 teenagers contract sexually transmitted diseases
500 adolescents begin using drugs
1,000 adolescents begin drinking alcohol
135,000 kids bring guns or other weapons to school
3,610 teens are assaulted; 80 are raped
2,200 teens drop out of high school
6 teens commit suicide.[1]

With this type of assault on the young people of our nation every day, it's no wonder many seem to be confused or do not seem to be capable of making godly decisions. In fact, seventy percent of today's young people state that absolute truth does not even exist. Within the churches of America fifty-seven percent cannot even say that an objective standard of truth exists.[2] In addition to the violence and sin listed above, young people are exposed to sin of all kinds on television, in movies, on videos, in many of the books and magazines that are readily available, through peer pressure, on the Internet, and the list could go on and on.

Adults are assaulted with the same things. Though these media are not evil in and of themselves, they can easily become sources of temptation. Though there are many avenues through which we can be tempted, these should suffice to show that we live in a world filled with easy access to temptation and where it is permissible, and often encouraged, for people to engage in sinful behavior. For example, just because you are now in Christ doesn't mean that the sinful things you have seen on television in the past will no longer have an effect on the way that you think. Neither does it mean that movies, books, magazines, or your peer group will no longer have an impact on you. As a matter of fact, Jesus told us that our eyes are the windows of our body and the things that we allow to enter through them will determine whether we are filled with light or darkness (Luke 11:34–36).

So far all we have done is to state the nature of the problem. We have all had a lot of evil influences in our lives and just because we are now in Christ does not automatically make those influences or thought patterns disappear. Tomorrow we will start examining what it means to be wise about what is good.

Prayer:

Our Father in heaven,

As we enter this study, please help us to identify any areas in our lives where we are still be influenced by the world. Help us to identify any strongholds or walls that will need to come down so You can mold us to be more like Your blessed Son. Create a clean heart in us. Thank You. In the name of Jesus, Amen!

Dear Reader,

I think it's important for you to know a little about my life. When I was fourteen years old, my parents moved from Arkansas to Holland to preach the gospel there. So from the time I was fourteen until I graduated from high school at eighteen, I lived in a society that was extremely open with its sexuality, and I became addicted to pornography. That addiction was in many ways in control of my life for nearly twenty-five years. I believed the lies that our enemy tells. I believed the lie that says that I would be in bondage for the rest of my life and that there was no way out. Yes, I was still genuinely trying to live a Christian life, but because of my own sinful choices I was being torn between what the flesh wanted and what the

*Spirit desired. It wasn't until I came face to face with the truths that are presented in this book that I realized that God has provided **everything** that we need to overcome our sins, even our addictions. But I had to personalize that promise—He came to set me free! I no longer have to live in bondage. By God's grace, I've been set free! I'm not saying that I'm now perfect or that I am never tempted. That would be a lie. But, because of what God has provided, I'm no longer a slave to the things that used to totally dominate my life.*

Which sins have been in control in your life is not what is important; what counts is that God has provided everything you need to be free from sin. He wants to set you free. Please let Him!

Your Servant in Christ,
Mark Richardson

Food for thought:

- Study 2 Corinthians 10:3–6, Romans 1:24–32, Galatians 5:19–21, Revelation 21:8, and 1 Corinthians 6:9–11.
- Spend some time thinking about the sins listed in the passages above, and then ask the Lord to reveal to you if any of these are things that you struggle with.
- Once you have identified any strongholds there may be in your life, please ask the Lord to help you to tear them down and to help you to be completely victorious over these sins.

Day Two

Wise About What Is Good

Whenever a student of the Word of God truly desires to know God's heart on any given subject, it is a good idea to examine everything that God has said concerning that subject. Today we will take a close look at Bible passages dealing with what it means to be wise about what is good.

The writer of Psalm 119 had a great deal to say about knowing and applying the Word of God. In verse nine he answered the question about how a person can keep his ways pure. He went on to give some practical advice about how we can apply God's Word to our lives.

Psalm 119

"How can a young man keep his way pure? By living according to your word" (Ps. 119:9)

In approaching a study concerning how to be wise about what is good and innocent about what is evil (Rom. 16:19) it makes sense to look at the true source of knowledge concerning what is good, namely, the Word of God. The question above asks how a young man (or anyone else) can keep his ways pure. The answer should always be the same as the one given above: pattern your life by the Word of God.

If you examine the entire chapter of Psalm 119 you will see in verse two that the writer reveals a very important matter concerning the heart. This verse tells us that people will be blessed if they will keep God's statutes and will "seek Him with all their heart." God is not looking for people who will half-heartedly give Him their allegiance. He wants people who seek Him with their whole hearts. That's why Moses wrote the command: "Love the LORD your God with all your heart and with all your soul and with all your strength" (Deut. 6:5) God wants His people to love Him first and foremost. He wants all of you, including your heart, your soul, and your strength. Half-hearted commitment does not bring any glory to God. Instead it tells the world that other things are more important in that person's life than service to his Creator. Deuteronomy 5:7 tells us, "You shall have no other gods before me." *God will not take second place.* He deserves and demands the number one spot—period.

So how can a person start making changes when they need to be made? The psalmist says his approach was to hide the Word in his heart in order that he might not sin against God (verse 11). By hiding the Word of God in one's heart (in other words by memorizing Scripture) one can begin growing in purity. The motivation for the memorization of Scripture is the desire to not sin against God. In verse twenty-four he goes on to say that God's statutes are his delight and his counselors. In verse thirty we see that he had set his heart on God's laws. He says in verse forty-eight that he meditated on God's decrees. In verse forty-nine he asks God to remind him of His Word. Each one of these passages lets us see how vital knowledge and active application of the Bible is to a person who really wants to please God.

"I gain understanding from your precepts; therefore I hate every wrong path" (Ps. 119:104). In an effort to know how to be wise about what is good, this verse tells us that the writer learned to hate things that were wrong by gaining understanding of the Lord's precepts. The very next verse (105) tells us that the Word of God is a lamp for our feet and a light for our path.

It would be such a blessing to the church today if all Christians had the same heart that the psalmist reveals when he asked God to open his eyes so that he could see wonderful things in God's law (Ps. 119:18).

One thing that I think is important to recognize from these passages is that it takes work. Throughout chapter 119, words and phrases like "seek," "meditate," "set my heart," etc., are used. There are a lot of other passages in this chapter that we could look at, but these suffice to show that what we need is not lip service but a genuine commitment to knowing and applying God's word.

Jesus also showed us by His example how we could apply these truths. When He was being tempted by Satan (Matt. 4:3–10), His answer to each temptation was virtually the same: "It is written." He knew what was good because He knew and followed God's Word.

On the mount of transfiguration the Father said, "This is my Son, whom I love; with him I am well pleased. Listen to him" (Matt. 17:5). To really understand what is good, we need to listen to this command and make sure we are listening to Jesus. In the Sermon on the Mount Jesus spent a great deal of time explaining what real goodness was all about. It was not simply a matter of going through some external rituals. It was not a matter of doing enough things right in an attempt to be righteous. Jesus spent much of this sermon telling the people that what God is really looking for is a heart that is obedient to Him. In fact, He begins the sermon with the words "Blessed are the poor in spirit" (Matt. 5:3). The concept of being poor in spirit is one that shows the condition of heart that the Father is looking for. He is looking for people who recognize that they need Him. D. Martyn Lloyd-Jones describes poverty of spirit as a mountain needing to be climbed and a recognition that a person is powerless to climb that mountain on his own.[3]

In Matthew 5:4 Jesus said, "Blessed are those who mourn." Again, Jesus is dealing with the heart. God is looking for people who not only recognize their need for Him, but who also realize that they are sinners and mourn because of that fact. Jesus is telling us that the people who are ultimately pleasing to God are those who recognize that they are sinful and who know they need God's grace and mercy if they are to have any hope.

In Matthew 5:5 He said, "Blessed are the meek," and in verse six He said, "Blessed are those who hunger and thirst for righteousness." Now we can see what it takes to be wise about what is good. Not only must the attitude of the heart be one of meekness, poverty of spirit, and mourning, but it must also be one of hungering and thirsting for righteousness (Matt. 5:3–6). When a person is physically hungry or thirsty, the natural response is to get something to eat or drink. That is what is being described here in the spiritual realm. Jesus is saying that when a person has the same burning desire for righteousness that he has when he is hungry for food, he will go to just as much effort to obtain righteousness that he would to get food in order to fill his stomach. If the Christian wants to be wise about good, then cultivating that hunger and thirst for righteousness is crucial.

In the eighth verse Jesus deals with another vital issue: "Blessed are the pure in heart, for they will see God." Purity of heart is ultimately what this book is all about. Purity of heart is a call to unmixed motives that seek only the will of God.

Later in this same sermon Jesus told His audience that their righteousness had to surpass that of the Pharisees and teachers of the law if they wanted to enter the kingdom of heaven (Matt. 5:20). If we were to go through the New Testament and study the problem with the Pharisees, we would learn that the problem was not necessarily what they taught, but what they did. They would often say many of the right things, but their actions and hearts were a different matter (Matt. 23:25–28). However, Jesus tells us that God is not interested in people who merely *say* they are His followers (Matt. 7:21). God commands people to love Him with all their heart, soul, mind, and strength (Deut. 6:3–4; Mark 12:30).

As Jesus continued His sermon He also taught a valuable lesson concerning how a person can protect himself from evil. "The eye is the lamp of the body. If your eyes are good, your whole body will be full of light. But if your eyes are bad, your whole body will be full of darkness. If then the light within you is darkness, how great is that darkness" (Matt. 6:22–23). Each person has control over what he will allow his eyes to dwell on. Though there will certainly be times when ugly and vile things are unexpectedly thrust in front of our eyes, this does not mean that we have to continue to look. Job went so far as to make a covenant with his eyes so that he would not look lustfully at a girl (Job 31:1). We will examine this concept in much more detail on another day, but this passage shows at least one very practical thing that can be done to return to innocence: We can commit to allowing our eyes to dwell only on things that are true, noble, right, pure, lovely, admirable, or praiseworthy (Phil. 4:8).

Paul talks about the importance of a person's mindset in the eighth chapter of Romans. "For those who live according to the flesh set their minds on the things of the flesh, but those who live according to the Spirit set their minds on the things of the Spirit" (Rom. 8:5 RSV). He goes on to say, "For the mind set on the flesh is death, but the mind set on the Spirit is life and peace, because the mind set on the flesh is hostile toward God; for it does not subject itself to the law of God, for it is not even able to do so, and those who are in the flesh cannot please God" (Rom. 8:6–8 NASB). So, in addition to the things that a person allows himself to look at, it is important what a person allows himself to think about.

Paul added even more insight into being wise about good when he wrote to the church at Colossae: "Since, then, you have been raised with Christ, set your hearts on things about where Christ is seated at the right hand of God. Set your minds on things above, not on earthly things. For you died, and your life is now hidden with Christ in God" (Col. 3:1–3). Christians are encouraged to set their minds on those things that are "heavenly."

James added more insight into this mindset when he wrote, "You adulteresses, do you not know that friendship with the world is hostility toward God? Therefore whoever wishes to be a friend of the world makes himself an enemy of God. Or do you think that the Scripture speaks to no purpose: 'He jealously desires the Spirit which He has made to dwell in us'?" (James 4:4–5 NASB). John added even more insight when he penned these words:

> Do not love the world nor the things in the world. If anyone loves the world, the love of the Father is not in him. For all that is in the world, the lust of the flesh and the lust of the eyes and the boastful pride of life, is not from the Father, but is from the world. (1 John 2:15–16)

James also wrote telling people to "get rid of all moral filth and the evil that is so prevalent and humbly accept the word planted in you, which can save you. Do not merely listen to the word, and so deceive yourselves. Do what it says" (James 1:21–22).

These passages give us a general overview concerning a wise approach to goodness and morality. In the days ahead we will examine what the Scriptures say on the subjects of wisdom, goodness, innocence and evil. Then we will start looking at some practical things that we can do to apply what we're studying.

Food for thought:

- Look back through the passages we've examined today that talk about what is good; then spend some time contemplating what you can do to increase these things in your life.
- After you have identified the areas you need to grow in, spend time studying and praying about those things specifically and asking the Lord to show you what you can do to apply the things you're learning to your daily walk with Christ.

Committing to Innocence

DAY THREE

The Value and Importance of Wisdom

Wisdom calls aloud in the street,
    she raises her voice in the public squares:
at the head of the noisy streets she cries out,
    in the gateways of the city she makes her speck:
How long will you simple ones love your simple ways?
    How long will mockers delight in mockery
    and fools hate knowledge?
If you had responded to my rebuke,
    I would have poured out my heart to you
    and made my thoughts known to you.
But since you rejected me when I called
    and no one gave heed when I stretched out my hand,
since you ignored all my advice
    and would not accept my rebuke,
I in turn will laugh at your disaster;
    I will mock when calamity overtakes you—
when calamity overtakes you like a storm,
    when disaster sweeps over you like a whirlwind,
    when distress and trouble overwhelm you.
Then they will call to me but I will not answer;
    they will look for me but will not find me.
Since they hated knowledge
    and did not choose to fear the LORD,
since they would not accept my advice
    and spurned my rebuke,
they will eat the fruit of their ways
    and be filled with the fruit of their schemes.
For the waywardness of the simple will kill them,
    and the complacency of fools will destroy them;
but whoever listens to me will live to safety
    and be at ease, without fear of harm. (Prov. 1:20–33)

This passage tells us how important and valuable wisdom really is. Without it, a person is not equipped to deal with calamity when it strikes. The significant thing to remember is that wisdom is something that requires advance preparation. It is at this point that most of us fail. It is when we do not prepare ahead of time that we fail when we are put to the test. The truly wise person does not wait until the calamity arises but has already laid a foundation to build on while wisdom was available. Wisdom called in the street (Prov. 1:20) but those who were unwilling to listen were the ones who were overtaken by disaster (Prov. 1:26).

Solomon spent a lot of time telling his son just how important this issue of wisdom really is. Listen to these words:

> Get wisdom, get understanding, do not forget my words or swerve from them. Do not forsake wisdom, and she will protect you; love her, and she will watch over you. Wisdom is supreme; therefore get wisdom. Though it cost you all you have, get understanding. Esteem her, and she will exalt you; embrace her, and she will honor you. She will set a garland of grace on your head and present you with a crown of splendor. Listen, my son, accept what I say, and the years of your life will be many. I guide you in the way of wisdom and lead you along straight paths. (Prov. 4:5–11)

The seventh verse is especially strong in presenting just how vital this issue is: "wisdom is supreme; therefore get wisdom." Solomon is telling his son, and anyone else who is willing to listen, to do whatever it takes to gain wisdom and understanding. Wisdom for the believer today is just as important as it was when Solomon wrote these words.

"The fear of the LORD is the beginning of wisdom, and knowledge of the Holy One is understanding" (Prov. 9:10). Wisdom starts with the fear of the Lord and knowledge of Him.

In their books about knowing and experiencing God, Henry Blackaby and Claude King tell us that there are seven realities of truly experiencing God. These realities are:

1. God is always at work around you.
2. God pursues a continuing love relationship with you that is real and personal.
3. God invites you to become involved with Him in His work.
4. God speaks by the Holy Spirit through the Bible, prayer, circumstances, and the church to reveal Himself, His purposes, and His ways.
5. God's invitation for you to work with Him always leads you to a crisis of belief that requires faith and action.
6. You must make major adjustments in your life to join God in what He is doing.
7. You come to know God by experience as you obey Him and He accomplishes His work through you.[4]

In the books and workbooks that Blackaby and King have written they talk a lot about coming to know God not just in your head but in your heart and experience. As a person begins to experience the truths contained in the seven realities listed above, he will come to know God by experience.

Solomon told his son that wisdom is better than gold and understanding is more precious than silver (Prov. 16:16). He then said, "He who gets wisdom loves his own soul." He also said that wisdom begins with the fear of the Lord (Prov. 9:10).

Seeking Wisdom

> My son, if you accept my words and store up my commands within you, turning your ear to wisdom and applying your heart to understanding, and if you call out for insight and cry aloud for understanding, and if you look for it as for silver and search for it as for hidden treasure, then you will understand the fear of the LORD and find the knowledge of God. For the LORD gives wisdom, and from his mouth come knowledge and understanding. (Prov. 2:1–6)

Solomon was telling his son not only that wisdom is something good, but that it should be actively pursued. Turn your ear to it. "Applying your heart," "call out," and "cry aloud" are all phrases that show that wisdom and understanding require work (Prov. 2:2–3). When Paul tells Christians to learn to be wise about what is good, we can be confident that the effort required for growing in this wisdom will certainly be worth the effort required for gaining it.

The Fear of the Lord

> A wise man fears the LORD and shuns evil. (Prov. 14:16)

> The fear of the LORD teaches a man wisdom, and humility comes before honor. (Prov. 15:33)

> The fear of the LORD is the beginning of wisdom; all who follow his precepts have good understanding. To him belongs eternal praise. (Ps. 111:10)

C.F. Keil and F. Delitzsch, in their commentary on the Old Testament, describe the fear of the Lord as "that careful, thoughtful, self-mistrusting reserve which flows from the reverential awe of God."[5] What a wonderful description! Because of reverential awe, the Christian should strive to understand the precepts of God. This is not motivation by terror, but rather a declaration of God's awesome power and might as well as His majesty. Christian service flows out of reverence for Him.

Learning to be wise about what is good must begin with knowledge of the only one that is good, namely, God (Mark 10:18).

Wisdom Comes From God

God appeared to Solomon in a dream and told him to ask for whatever he wanted (1 Kings 3:5). In the following passage we find out what Solomon asked for and the answer that he received from God:

> Now, O LORD my God, you have made your servant king in place of my father David. But I am only a little child and do not know how to carry out my duties. Your servant is here among the people you have chosen, a great people, too numerous to count or number. So give your servant a discerning heart to govern your people and to distinguish between right and wrong. For who is able to govern this great people of yours?"
>
> The LORD was pleased that Solomon had asked for this. So God said to him, "Since you have asked for this and not for long life or wealth for yourself, nor have asked for the death of your enemies but for discernment in administering justice, I will do what you have asked. I will give you a wise and discerning heart, so that there will never have been anyone like you, nor will there ever be. Moreover, I will give you what you have not asked for—both riches and honor—so that in your lifetime you will have no equal among kings. (1 Kings 3:6–8)

God gave Solomon wisdom and very great insight, and a breadth of understanding as measureless as the sand on the seashore. Solomon's wisdom was greater than the wisdom of all the men of the East, and greater than all the wisdom of Egypt (1 Kings 4:29–30).

> If any of you lacks wisdom, he should ask God, who gives generously to all without finding fault, and it will be given to him. But when he asks, he must believe and not doubt, because he who doubts is like a wave of the sea, blown and tossed by the wind. That man should not think he will receive anything from the Lord; he is a double-minded man, unstable in all he does. (James 1:5–8)

When we examine the passages listed above, we see an important concept presented, namely, that true wisdom comes from God. Solomon asked for it and received it. James tells us that if we will ask for it and not doubt that we will receive it as well.

> But as for you, continue in what you have learned and have become convinced of, because you know those from who you learned it, and how from infancy you have known the holy Scriptures, which are able to make you wise for salvation through faith in Christ Jesus. All Scripture is God-breathed and is useful for teaching, rebuking, correcting and training in righteousness, so that the man of God may be thoroughly equipped for every good work. (2 Tim. 3:14–17)

James also tells us there are two kinds of wisdom. There is the kind of wisdom that the world practices, which will harbor envy and selfish motives in their hearts. James refers to this as worldly wisdom. The other wisdom he identifies is the wisdom that comes from heaven. He describes it as that wisdom that is pure, peace-loving, considerate, submissive, full of mercy and good fruit, impartial and sincere (James 3:13–18).

Worldly wisdom is full of bitterness and envy; it is unspiritual and its source is the devil. If we will open our eyes and look around we can easily see worldly wisdom displayed every day. The world tells people to "look out for number one." Worldly wisdom promotes selfishness and draws people away from God. But "the wisdom that comes from heaven" (James 3:17) helps the believer to be wise about what is good.

> Therefore everyone who hears these words of mine and puts them into practice is like a wise man who built his house on the rock. The rain came down, the streams rose, and the winds blew and beat against that house; yet it did not fall, because it had its foundation on the rock. But everyone who hears these words of mine and does not put them into practice is like a foolish man who built his house on sand. The rain came down, the streams rose, and the winds blew and beat against that house, and it fell with a great crash." (Matt. 7:24–27)

This lesson of preparation is also shown in Matthew 25:1–13 when Jesus talked about the wise and foolish virgins. Wisdom was shown by their making advance preparation. Jesus tells the people in Matthew seven that the wise person will put His words into practice, but the foolish person will not. The same was true of the ten virgins. Some of them made preparation while the others did not. Worldly wisdom simply lives for the moment, but true wisdom recognizes that there is much more to life than simply living for today. As Christians our citizenship is in heaven (Phil. 3:20) and we should be preparing for it by the way that we live. In 1 John 3:2–3 we read, "Dear friends, now we are children of God, and what we will be has not yet been made known. But we know that when he appears, we shall be like him, for we shall see him as he is. Everyone who has this hope in him purifies himself, just as he is pure." In other words, if you are serious about going to heaven, you will be serious about growing in purity.

The interesting thing about the passages above is that they show how our actions clearly demonstrate which type of wisdom we are following.

Wisdom and the Tongue

> When words are many, sin is not absent, but he who holds his tongue is wise (Prov. 10:19).

> A wise man's heart guides his mouth, and his lips promote instruction. (Prov. 16:23)

Jesus said it this way: "For out of the overflow of the heart the mouth speaks. The good man brings good things out of the good stored up in him, and the evil man brings evil things out of the evil stored up in him" (Matt. 12:34b–35). It is what fills your heart that determines the words that come out of your mouth. Proverbs 17:28 says, "Even a fool is thought wise if he keeps silent, and discerning if he holds his tongue."

This passage has sometimes been paraphrased "Better to be silent and thought a fool than to speak and remove all doubt."

What we learn from these passages is simply stated in this way: Wisdom guards the tongue. If we want to be truly wise people, we will fill our hearts with those things that are good so that what comes from the overflow of the heart will be good as well.

If we tie together all that we've examined, we can sum it up like this: Wisdom comes from God (James 1:5–8). It begins with reverence and awe for our Creator (Ps. 111:10). The wisdom that comes from God will change our conduct and our speech (James 3:13–18) and has a tremendous amount of value (Prov. 1:20–33).

Tomorrow we will start examining what the Bible says about being good.

Food for thought:

- In James 1:5 we're told to ask for wisdom and that God will give it.
- Spend time asking the Lord to give you the wisdom you need to grow in faith, in love and in purity of heart.
- Beware the trap of trying to utilize only your own wisdom and strength to produce the growth that is needed. We are incapable of producing these changes based solely on our human strength.

Day Four

Good

The biblical concept of moral and spiritual goodness stands in contrast with much of the world's view of goodness. The biblical concept can be summarized as follows:

A. God is good. He is morally perfect and wonderfully generous.
B. God's works are good. His works reveal His wisdom and power.
C. God's gifts are good. They express His generosity, and provide for the well being of His followers.
D. God's commands are good. They express His moral perfection and His character and by showing us how to please Him, show us the path of true blessing.
E. Obedience to His commands is good. God is pleased by it, and those who obey Him will profit from that obedience.[6]

No One Is Good

> All have turned aside, they have together become corrupt; there is no one who does good, not even one. (Ps. 14:3)

> But now a righteousness from God, apart from law, has been made known, to which the Law and the Prophets testify. This righteousness from God comes through faith in Jesus Christ to all who believe. There is no difference, for all have sinned and fall short of the glory of God, and are justified freely by his grace through the redemption that came by Christ Jesus. (Rom. 3:21–24)

In both of those passages the same concept is clearly stated: all have sinned. (The same thing is stated in Romans 3:23.) In fact when we look at the Scriptures, we learn that the only one who has not sinned is Jesus Christ:

> Therefore, since we have a great high priest who has gone through the heavens, Jesus the Son of God, let us hold firmly to the faith we profess. For we do not have a high priest who is unable to sympathize with our weaknesses, but we have one who has been tempted in every way, just as we are—yet was without sin. Let us then approach the throne of grace with confidence, so that we may receive mercy and find grace to help us in our time of need. (Heb. 4:14–16)

We have a high priest who has gone through temptation yet *did not sin*. Since Jesus shared in our humanity (Heb. 2:14–15), He was certainly qualified to step in and take our place. He did not sin, but everyone else has (Rom. 3:23). Because we sin, we cannot classify ourselves as being morally good. The only one who qualifies for that is God. In the first chapter of John (as well as many other passages) we see that Jesus is God. Listen to his words:

> In the beginning was the Word, and the Word was with God, and the Word was God. He was with God in the beginning. Through him all things were made; without him nothing was made that has been made. In him was life, and that life was the light of men . . . The Word became flesh and made his dwelling among us. We have seen his glory, the glory of the One and Only, who came from the Father, full of grace and truth. (John 1:1–4,14)

The Lord is Good

> Trust and see that the Lord is good; blessed is the man who takes refuge in him. (Ps. 34:8)

> For the LORD is good and his love endures forever; his faithfulness continues through all generations. (Ps. 100:5)

Josh McDowell does a wonderful job of explaining that God is the ultimate source of morality. In the book *Right From Wrong* he describes the revelation of morality in the following way: "God's Word is filled with *precepts*—commands put there for our good. *Principles* are the 'whys' behind the precepts, and the *person* behind the principles is God Himself. As we move from *precept* to *principle*, it leads to the very *person* of God. It is through the Test of Truth that we compare our attitudes and actions to God's character and nature."[7] (We will look at this process again on another day.)

Knowledge of Good is Revealed

Before Adam and Eve sinned by eating of the tree of knowledge of good and evil, they didn't know what sin was. All they knew was good. It was when they sinned that their eyes were opened. Now they knew what sin was and what good was. They had to face the consequences of their actions, and they were cast out of the garden and death entered the world (Gen. 3).

It is an amazing thing to realize that sinful man can know a pure and holy God. Yet in His mercy and grace He has chosen to reveal Himself to us. Apart from that revelation, we would have no way of knowing Him. God has revealed His power and might in the splendor of what He has created (Rom. 1:20), but He has revealed much more than that by sending His Son (John 1:18) and by giving us His Word, which can make us wise for salvation (2 Tim. 3:15).

Good Fruit

> Watch out for false prophets. They come to you in sheep's clothing, but inwardly they are ferocious wolves. By their fruit you will recognize them. Do people pick grapes from thorn-bushes, or figs from thistles? Likewise every good tree bears good fruit, but a bad tree

bears bad fruit. A good tree cannot bear bad fruit, and a bad tree cannot bear good fruit. (Matt. 7:15–18)

Trees are judged by the fruit that they bear, just as people's lives are judged by the fruit that they bear. The goal is to make our lives and our fruit good. If we want to get good out of our lives, it's important that we fill ourselves with those things that are good and wholesome. In fact, Jesus taught us that it's out of the overflow of the heart that the mouth speaks (Matt. 12:34). So if we want to be sure that our hearts are filled with those things that are good, we need to make sure we are only allowing those things to enter. (We will be looking much closer at this concept later.)

Do Good

Now it is time to examine what the Scriptures teach about doing what is good.

> Do what is right and good in the Lord's sight, so that it may go well with you. (Deut. 6:18a)

> Be careful to obey all these regulations I am giving you, so that it may always go well with you and your children after you, because you will be doing what is good and right in the eyes of the Lord your God. (Deut. 12:2)

This passage makes a very important statement, namely that when people obey the Lord's commands they are doing what is good and right in God's eyes. Jesus took this idea even further when He stated that if anyone loves Him, that person would obey His commands (John 14:21). The flip side of this coin is also true: though a person may claim love for Jesus, if there is no real love for Him there won't be any obedience either. Just as faith produces action (James 2:14–26), here we see that love demands obedience.

"This is what the Lord says: 'Stand at the crossroads and look; ask for the ancient paths, ask where the good way is, and walk in it, and you will find rest for your souls'" (Jer. 6:16a). It is not enough to just say that a person desires to do good, but each person needs to also learn to actively pursue that which is good, and once the path is found, to follow it.

Paul wrote about doing good in Ephesians 2:10 when he said, "For we are God's workmanship, created in Christ Jesus to do good works, which God prepared in advance for us to do." There are certain works that God prepared in advance for Christians to do. Even though Paul stated in Ephesians 2:9 that we are not saved by doing works, he does not leave room for the view that a person can faithfully follow Christ and still not do anything. In other words we do not work in order to be saved, but we do work because we are saved. Faith and love are both demonstrated by action. Jesus also touched on this concept when he said that it is not the person who says "Lord, Lord" who is going to be saved, but the one who does the will of God (Matt. 7:21).

> Let us not become weary in doing good, for at the proper time we will reap a harvest if we do not give up. Therefore, as we have opportunity, let us do good to all people, especially to those who belong to the family of believers. (Gal. 6:9–10)

Do not grow weary in doing those things that are good! What a wonderful command. It is also accompanied by a wonderful promise. If a person does not grow weary in doing good, and does not give up, he will reap a harvest. Paul added even more details on this subject when he wrote to Titus: "Tell the older women to teach what is good" (Titus 2:3). Set an example "by doing what is good" (Titus 2:7). God's people need to learn to be eager to "do what is good" (Titus 2:14). Christians should always be "ready to do whatever is good" (Titus 3:1). They also need to "be careful to devote themselves to doing what is good" (Titus 3:8) and "learn to engage in good deeds to meet pressing needs, that they may not be unfruitful" (Titus 3:14 NASB).

Here is another beautiful promise: If God's people will learn to devote themselves to that which is good, and if they will learn to engage in meeting pressing needs, then they will bear fruit (Titus 3:14). If you want to be sure that you are going to bear good fruit in your life, get your eyes off of yourself and learn how to meet other people's needs.

Summary: We are all sinners (Rom. 3:23). God is the only one who is truly good (Matt. 19:17). Knowledge of good and knowledge of God are both revealed in His Word (2 Tim. 3:16–17; John 1:18).

It is God's will for you to be wise about what is good and innocent about what is evil (Rom. 16:19). Tomorrow we will look at what the Scriptures teach about being innocent.

Food for thought:

- If we simplify the concept of good we could ask of any situation or action, Is it like God?
- Our goal is to grow to become more godly in our lives.
- Spend time considering who God is—His goodness, His mercy, His compassion, etc.
- Pray that God will enable you to grow daily to be more like Him.

Day Five

Innocent

The various ways that the word "innocent" is used in the Old Testament include some of the following definitions: just, pure, without a cause, pure (in a moral sense), to be clean, and blameless.[8] We have already seen that no one is truly innocent, because we have all sinned (Rom. 3:23). What a wonderful blessing to know that Christ's righteousness has been credited to our account (Rom. 4:23–24). However, we still have the responsibility to grow in purity of heart. In fact, John wrote,

> Dear friends, now we are children of God, and what we will be has not yet been made known. But we know that when he appears, we shall be like him, for we shall see him as he is. Everyone who has this hope in him purifies himself, just as he is pure. (1 John 3:2–3).

Everyone who has the hope that he will see Jesus upon His return will purify himself.

As we look at the various passages in Scripture that tell us about innocence, keep in mind that the major topic we are examining is the goal of learning to be wise about what is good and innocent about things that are evil.

> If a man is found slain, lying in a field in the land the LORD your God is giving you to possess, and it is not known who killed him, your elders and judges shall go out and measure the distance from the body to the neighboring town. Then the elders of the town nearest the body shall take a heifer that has never been worked and has never worn a yoke and lead her down to a valley that has not been plowed or planted and where there is a flowing stream. There in the valley they are to break the heifer's neck. The priests, the sons of Levi, shall

step forward, for the LORD your God has chosen them to minister and to pronounce blessings in the name of the LORD and to decide all cases of dispute and assault. Then all the elders of the town nearest the body shall wash their hands over the heifer whose neck was broken in the valley, and they shall declare; "Our hands did not shed this blood, nor did our eyes see it done. Accept this atonement for your people Israel, whom you have redeemed, O LORD, and do not hold your people guilty of the blood of an innocent man." And the bloodshed will be atoned for. So you will purge from yourselves the guilt of shedding innocent blood, since you have done what is right in the eyes of the LORD. (Deut. 21:1–9)

In this passage we see how God made provision for an entire town when a dead body was found but it was not known who killed him. If the town followed the prescribed directions, they would purge themselves of the guilt of shedding innocent blood.

"Moreover, Manasseh also shed so much innocent blood that he filled Jerusalem from end to end—besides the sin that he had caused Judah to commit, so that they did evil in the eyes of the LORD" (2 Kings 21:16).[9] Manasseh killed a lot of people who were described as innocent. He did not kill them because he wanted revenge for some kind of crime or because they had done something to him. He killed innocent people.

Solomon said that all of a man's ways seem innocent to him, but the Lord weighs the motives (Prov. 16:2). He also said there "is a way that seems right to a man, but in the end it leads to death" (Prov. 14:12; 16:25). Just because a person thinks something is right does not make it so. Many people in recent years have lived by the philosophy "If it feels good, do it." But, as Solomon points out, just because it feels right doesn't make it right. Feelings do not make the person innocent. God is looking at the motives in our hearts.

Jesus told his disciples to be "innocent like doves" (Matt 10:16). We, like the disciples, are to strive to be totally free of guilt. That's the goal. It's the same thing Paul was referring to when he said that we should strive to be "innocent about what is evil" (Rom. 16:19).

The common theme of the passages discussing innocence is that people were either *not guilty* of a sin or crime or they were *not held accountable* for the sin or crime. They were considered innocent. The word innocent also carries with it the idea of being "unmixed." We should be living in a way that does not contribute anything to growing in evil, a way that is totally committed to growing ever closer to our God. Tomorrow we will examine what the Bible describes as things that are evil.

Food for thought:

- The more specific you can be in identifying the areas in your life where innocence has been lost, the more effective you will be in confronting and overcoming them.
- We've already looked at some of these concepts before, but just because we may have identified them doesn't mean that the thoughts and struggles have now simply vanished. Growth is a process.
- Please spend massive amounts of time in prayer, in study, talking with strong Christian brothers and sisters about the areas you need to grow in, and searching for ways to daily grow to be more and more pure in heart.

Day Six

Evil

If we were to travel back in time to find out when evil first showed its ugly head, we would end up in the Garden of Eden. The Lord had made all kinds of trees to grow in the garden. In the middle of the garden were both the tree of life and the tree of the knowledge of good and evil. God told Adam and Eve they could eat of any of the trees in the garden except for the tree of knowledge of good and evil. When Adam and Eve sinned, their eyes were opened and they gained knowledge of what sin was. At that point they realized that they were naked and they tried to hide from God. Because of their sin they were kicked out of the garden and death entered the picture, just as God had told them (Gen. 2:9–3:24).

Evil Thoughts

Time passed, and as the population began to grow, so did the desire to sin. It got to the point that wickedness and violence dominated the thoughts of men. This is when God looked at mankind and grieved because of how vile the world had become. "The LORD saw how great man's wickedness on the earth had become, and that every inclination of the thoughts of his heart was only evil all the time" (Gen. 6:5). Because of the sin that reigned in the lives of these men and women, God destroyed the world with a flood (Gen. 7:13–24). God then gave a sign to Noah that He would never destroy the world with a flood again (Gen. 9:12–16). But by looking at the flood and the reason for it, we can see just how much sin truly hurts God. He was so grieved by man's sinfulness that He destroyed them (Gen. 7:21).

Purge the Evil

The book of Deuteronomy nine times uses a phrase that tells us a lot about the heart of God. The phrase is "purge the evil" (Deut. 13:5; 17:7,12; 19:19; 21:21; 22:21,22,24; 24:7). Nine times God told the children of Israel to get rid of the evil. In Deuteronomy 13:4 they were told that they were to follow God and keep His commands. In verse five they were told that any person that tried to turn them away from God had to be purged from among them. Chapter 17:2–7 is about people who were worshipping other gods. Verse twelve is about a man who shows contempt for a judge or priest. By doing this he is rejecting the authorities God had put in place. As we look at the various passages we see a common theme: God must have preeminence! God would not allow evil in the camp.

Israel Did Evil

Throughout the book of Judges we see the children of Israel going through a terrible cycle of sinning against God, crying out for help, God sending a deliverer, Israel experiencing a time of peace, and then the cycle starting again (Judg. 2:11; 3:7,12; 4:1; 6:1; 10:6; 13:1). What was the evil thing that Israel kept going back to? They turned away from God and served the Baals (Judg. 2:11). All through the Bible we see that God's heart is always the same on this issue: "You shall have no other gods before me" (Deut. 5:7). This command is one that touches every area of our lives. Nothing can come before God! That is why Jesus told His followers that the greatest command was to love the Lord with all your heart, soul, mind and strength (Mark 12:30).

Some Commands Concerning Evil

Do not be wise in your own eyes, fear the LORD and shun evil. (Prov. 3:7)

> Hate evil, love good. (Amos 5:15)

In Amos 5:14 we read the words "seek good, not evil, that you may live." These commands illustrate the heart of God concerning how important good and evil are to Him and how much He desires (demands) that His people keep themselves from evil and pursue a life of goodness and purity. He wants His people not only to strive for those things that are good, but also to stay away from and even to hate those things that are evil.[10] The reason for this is that He is holy and wants His followers to be the same. (Lev. 11:45).

> Whoever would love life and see good days must keep his tongue from evil and his lips from deceitful speech. He must turn from evil and do good; he must seek peace and pursue it. For the eyes of the Lord are on the righteous and his ears are attentive to their prayers, but the face of the Lord is against those who do evil. (1 Pet. 3:10–12)

Upon careful examination of this text we can see that Peter is telling God's elect (1 Peter 1:1) that the overall direction of one's life is a personal decision. Peter is not dealing with the subject of salvation by works, but is dealing with which path a person chooses to follow. Each person can choose to seek and pursue peace, or he can choose to continue to do evil rather than striving to do that which is good.

Miscellaneous References to Evil

The scriptures refer to "evil spirits," "evil deeds," and "evil desires." Though we could go into a lengthy study of each of these, that would detract from our overall study goal, which is to learn to be wise about what is good and innocent about what is evil. The main thing that we need to keep in mind is this: Anything that is contrary to God's heart is evil.

Evil versus Good

Paul told the church at Rome that wrath and anger awaited people who were self-seeking and who rejected the truth (Rom. 2:8). He also told them that they should hate what is evil and cling to what is good (12:9). When he wrote to the church at Corinth he told them that his desire was for them to be infants in regard to evil (1 Cor. 14:20). In 1 Thessalonians 5:22 he said to "avoid every kind of evil."

We saw in Genesis how sin separated man from God. That hasn't changed. Evil (sin) kills. Our sin is what brought about the necessity of Christ's death on the cross. Man's sin brought about the flood, the death of Christ (1 Cor. 15:1–4) and judgment for those who do not obey the gospel (2 Thess. 1:6–10).

Though it may not be considered socially or politically correct to talk about sin, we need to realize that God is the one who created us and that He (and He alone) has the right to determine what is or is not evil behavior. In the various places where He spoke about hell, Jesus taught us about the seriousness of dying in a lost condition (Matt. 5:22,29,30; 10:38; 18:9; 23:15,33; Mark 9:43,45,47; Luke 12:5; 16:23). Sin is serious; that is why Jesus died. As we consider the subject of evil in the Bible, we can easily see why Paul would admonish the church to be "innocent about evil" (Rom. 16:19).

The rest of this book will deal with the practical side of what it means to be wise about good and innocent about evil (Rom. 16:19).

Food for thought:

- We live in a society that pretty much says that there is no such thing as sin or evil. However, as we read the Bible, we see that God describes certain things as sinful and evil. We must make sure that we are going by God's definition and not the world's.
- As you identify areas of sin in your life, repent! Confess those sins to a brother or sister in Christ (James 5:16) and confess them to the Lord, who will forgive you (1 John 1:9) Then replace the sinful behavior with things that will draw you closer to God.

Raising the Standard

Day Seven

Living on a Higher Plane

Dear friends, now we are children of God, and what we will be has not yet been made known. But we know that when he appears, we shall be like him, for we shall see him as he is. Everyone who has this hope in him purifies himself, just as he is pure. (1 John 3:2–3). What a fantastic statement concerning Christian living. When Jesus appears, we will be like Him! *Everyone* who has the hope that he will be like Jesus purifies Himself.

The purpose for this entire study is to help each of us see how we can "return to innocence," or how we can develop a purer heart. What we are striving for is not the development of a holier-than-thou attitude, but learning to live a life that is far greater than what the world can possibly imagine. In fact, we are told in the book of Ephesians that whatever we can "ask or imagine" (3:20–21) God can do. If we can imagine living a life totally committed to serving our lord and savior Jesus Christ, God can enable us to live it. While purity and innocence are impossible for us as sinful people, they are not impossible for God, who places His Holy Spirit with us.[11]

Gary Oliver, in *The Seven Promises of a Promise Keeper*, describes a seven-step process to help people to conform to the likeness of Christ. He also states that simply desiring purity is not enough. To actually change requires a plan or action. Here is the action plan that he laid out:

Step 1: Make a decision.
Step 2: Choose to put first things first.
Step 3: Determine where the line is, then stay as far from the line as you can.
Step 4: Guard your heart.
Step 5: Guard your mind.
Step 6: Guard your eyes.
Step 7: Guard the little things.[12]

This is such a wonderful description of a plan for developing purity. It starts with a decision. The decision is then followed with a determination of where you are and where you want to be. Then he talks about defending yourself from evil influences. We will look at many of these items in much more detail in later chapters, but these steps do help to lay a good foundation for showing that growing in purity is possible.

Also in the same book, Tony Evans gives a marvelous description of what spiritual purity looks like:

First: The Spiritually pure man has divine continuity with the past.
Second: The Spiritually pure man is committed to raising his children.
Third: The Spiritually pure man earns respect.
Fourth: The Spiritually pure man is a man of mercy.
Fifth: The Spiritually pure man is a man of justice.

Sixth: The Spiritually pure man is a man of stability.
Seventh: The Spiritually pure man is a man of wisdom.[13]

Jesus started the Sermon on the Mount with the words "Blessed are the poor in spirit" (Matt. 5:3). The process for developing "spiritual purity" begins in the heart. It starts, as we see in Matthew 5:3, with poverty of spirit. In other words, we need God! We must learn to see and acknowledge just how much we really do need Him.

On a very practical level in our lives, the battle we fight is one between *truth* and *lies*. Jesus said, "If you hold to my teaching you are really my disciples. Then you will know the truth and the truth will set you free" (John 8:31–32 NIV). Later in the same chapter Jesus revealed the fact that Satan is the father of all lies (8:44). In our daily lives we need to constantly be examining whether the things that we are doing, seeing, and believing line up with the truth or if they are lies. Master the art of holding on to the teaching of Jesus and then "you will know the truth and the truth will set you free" (John 8:31–32 NIV). Always base your thoughts and actions on the truth, and you will be able to truly live life on a much higher plane.

The ultimate goal for the Christian, in this life, should be to grow daily to be more like Jesus. To do this we must live with our focus on Jesus. Tomorrow we will examine what it means to focus on Him.

Food for thought:

- Remember that Satan is a liar. He wants you to believe that you will have to struggle with defeat and bondage for the rest of your life.
- The more we can focus on the truth, the better off we will be for it really is the truth that sets us free (John 8:32).
- Spend some time meditating on the thought that Christ came to offer abundant life (John 10:10), not a life of constant defeat from our enemy.

Day Eight

Focusing on Jesus

O to be like Thee! Blessed Redeemer: This is my constant longing and prayer, Gladly I'll forfeit all of earth's treasures, Jesus, Thy perfect likeness to wear.

O to be like Thee! Full of compassion, Loving, forgiving, tender and kind, Helping the helpless, cheering the fainting, Seeking the wand'ring sinner to find.

O to be like Thee! Lowly in spirit, Holy and harmless, patient and brave: Meekly enduring cruel reproaches, Willing to suffer, others to save.

O to be like Thee! Lord, I am coming, Now to receive th' anointing divine: All that I am and have I am bringing; Lord, from this moment all shall be Thine.

Chorus:

O to be like Thee! O to be like Thee! Blessed Redeemer, pure as Thou art, Come in Thy sweetness, come in Thy fullness; Stamp Thine own image deep on my heart.[14]

Don McLaughlin, in his book *Heaven in the Real World*, states that heaven's purpose for people who have lost their likeness to the creator is to re-clothe them with Christ.[15] Charles Sheldon, in the book *In His Steps*, raises a powerful question in seeking a way to better follow Jesus. It is a simple, but very powerful question: "What would Jesus do?"[16] As disciples of Jesus striving to grow closer to Him, this question is a great tool for beginning to develop a mindset of Christ-likeness. Until that question can be answered, it will be impossible to behave as He would.

Max Lucado personalizes this question even more. "What if, for one day and one night, Jesus lived your life with His heart?"[17] Wow! Just think how much that day would be different from other days in your life. It is God's desire for you to think and act just like Jesus.

How did Jesus describe eternal life? "Now this is eternal life: that they may know you, the only true God, and Jesus Christ, whom you have sent" (John 17:3). Eternal life is knowing God and knowing Jesus. This is not just talking about having a casual acquaintance with God but true intimacy. It is through fellowship with Christ that we overcome the world.[18] Jesus said it this way:

> Remain in me, and I will remain in you. No branch can bear fruit by itself; it must remain in the vine. Neither can you bear fruit unless you remain in me. I am the vine, you are the branches. If a man remains in me and I in him, he will bear much fruit; apart from me you can do nothing. (John 15:4–5)

Oh, if we would all learn the truth of this statement. Apart from Jesus we can do nothing. Without His help we cannot be the kind of servants, givers, spouses, parents, or Christians we should be. While we proceed with this study we must keep in mind that our eyes must stay focused on Jesus. The second we try to grow on our own or try to mold ourselves is the second that we get onto the wrong path, because apart from Christ we cannot do it. Stay focused!

The writer of Hebrews wrote these words:

> Therefore, since we surrounded by such a great cloud of witnesses, let us throw off everything that hinders and the sin that so easily entangles, and let us run with perseverance the race marked out for us. Let us fix our eyes on Jesus, the author and perfector of our faith, who for the joy set before him endured such opposition from sinful men, so that you will not grow weary and lose heart. (Heb. 12:1–3)

Consider Him! Thomas à Kempis believed that our chief endeavor should be to meditate on the life of Jesus.[19] He then went on to say that the one who earnestly desires to understand the words of Christ must endeavor to conform his life wholly to the life of Christ. John wrote in 1 John 2:6, "Whoever claims to live in him must walk as Jesus did." We are called to follow Christ.

The passages we have looked at and the various authors we have quoted have been telling us that we must begin by getting our eyes off ourselves and putting them on Jesus. The believer needs to make the commitment to constantly be looking at Jesus. Or as the Hebrew writer put it—keep your eyes fixed on Jesus (Heb. 12:2).

As a practical way of staying focused on Christ, spend a great deal of time studying Matthew, Mark, Luke, and John. Look at the things that made Jesus happy, the things that made Him sad, the things that made Him angry, etc. Then spend time in earnest soul searching and prayer asking God to mold you daily to be more like Christ.

In addition to changing our focus from self to Christ, the Bible also tells us to get our eyes off of the present and to focus them on the eternal. We will examine this in more detail tomorrow.

Food for thought:

- Our focus in life as followers of Christ should be to grow to be more like Him.
- Spend time studying Matthew, Mark, Luke, and John and seeing all that you can about Jesus. Consider the things that made Him happy. What made Him sad? How did He spend His time? Who did He associate with? etc. The better you get to know Him, the clearer picture you have of what the Father is like (John 14:9).
- Spend some time praying about what areas in your life need to be molded to be more like Christ, and ask God to begin changing you to be more like Him.

Day Nine

Focusing on Heaven

This world is not my home,
I'm just a passing thru.
My treasures are laid up
somewhere beyond the blue;
The angels beckon me
from heaven's open door,
And I can't feel at home
in this world anymore.[20]

If a Christian's perspective is centered only on today, he is no different from the people of the world. Not only should our purpose in life be different from the world's, but our perspective should also be different. We should be heaven focused, not world focused. (By world focused I am referring to things that are worldly or that would fall into the categories of the lust of the flesh, the lust of the eyes, or the pride of life.)

> I want to know Christ and the power of his resurrection and the fellowship of sharing in his sufferings, becoming like him in his death, and so, somehow, to attain to the resurrection from the dead.
>
> Not that I have already obtained all this, or have already been made perfect, but I press on to take hold of that for which Christ Jesus took hold of me. Brothers, I do not consider myself yet to have taken hold of it. But one thing I do: Forgetting what is behind and straining toward what is ahead, I press on toward the goal to win the prize for which God has called me heavenward in Christ Jesus.

All of us who are mature should take such a view of things. And if on some point you think differently, that too God will make clear to you. Only let us live up to what we have already attained.

Join with others in following my example, brothers, and take not of those who live according to the pattern we gave you. For, as I have often told you before and now say again even with tears, many live as enemies of the cross of Christ. Their destiny is destruction, their god is their stomach, and their glory is in their shame. Their mind is on earthly things. But our citizenship is in heaven. And we eagerly await a Savior from there, the Lord Jesus Christ, who, by the power that enables him to bring everything under his control, will transform our lowly bodies so that they will be like his glorious body. (Phil. 3:10–21)

Our citizenship is in heaven! This verse expresses such a beautiful description of who we are as God's children. We are heavenly citizens. I have family members who were born in Holland though their parents are both U.S. citizens. When they turned eighteen they had the right to choose citizenship. They could choose to be citizens of Holland or of the United States. God offers people a choice of citizenship that is much more important than the choice my family faced. When we become Christians we are changed and we become citizens of heaven.

Though this concept, when taken to the extreme, can be used to avoid accepting earthly responsibility, that is not what is being referred to here or in Scripture. If you look at what the Bible says, God's people are taught to be responsible in every area of their lives. What we are talking about here is *mindset*. The Hebrew writer alluded to this concept when he wrote about the great people of faith who were longing for a "better country—a heavenly one" (Heb. 11:16).

In Ephesians 2:19 Paul wrote that Christians are a part of God's household. With these thoughts in mind we have even more reason to get excited about the statement that Jesus made in the book of John when he said,

Do not let your hearts be troubled. Trust in God; trust also in me. In my Father's house are many rooms; if it were not so, I would have told. I am going there to prepare a place for you. And if I go and prepare a place for you, I will come back and take you to be with me that you also may be where I am. (John 14:1–3)

Take comfort! Why? Jesus has gone to prepare a dwelling place in heaven for you. As God's children our perspective needs to be heavenward focused, not earthward.

As Christians struggle with being torn between heaven and earth, we see another part of the issue that Paul described in Romans chapter eight as the battle between the carnal (of the flesh) and the spiritual. We will take a look at that conflict tomorrow.

Food for thought:

- As Paul told the church in Philippi, we are now citizens of heaven. Though we certainly need to be sure we still fulfill our earthly obligations, our major focus in life needs to change.
- As you interact with others, focus on heaven. What can you do to help them to get there with you?
- As you consider making changes in your life, always make decisions and changes based on how they will affect your relationship with God. Will the changes help you or the people around you to draw closer to the Lord? If not, don't do it.

Day Ten

Flesh vs. Spirit

Paul talked, in Romans chapters seven and eight, about a battle that takes place within each individual believer. The true war within is between the flesh (the self-oriented soul) and the Spirit.[21]

> For we know that the Law is spiritual; but I am of flesh, sold into bondage to sin. For that which I am doing, I do not understand; for I am not practicing what I *would* like to *do,* but I am doing the very thing I hate. But if I do the very thing I do not wish *to do,* I agree with the Law, *confessing* that it is good. So now, no longer am I the one doing it, but sin which indwells me. For I know that nothing good dwells in me, that is, in my flesh; for the wishing is present in me, but the doing of the good *is* not. For the good that I wish, I am no longer the one doing it, but sin which dwells in me. I find then the principle that evil is present in me, the one who wishes to do good. For I joyfully concur with the law of God in the inner man, but I see a different law in the members of my body, waging war against the law of my mind, and making me a prisoner of the law of sin which is in my members. Wretched man that I am! Who will set me free from the body of this death? Thanks be to God through Jesus Christ our Lord! So then, on the one hand I myself with my mind am serving the law of God, but on the other, with my flesh the law of sin. (Rom. 7:14–25 NASB)

Two conflicting roles are discussed in the passage above. One role wants to follow law; the other is opposed to the following of law. The ancient Greeks and Romans discussed this concept a great deal. Ovid, in *Metamorphoses,* described this conflict this way: "Desire persuades me one way, reason another. I see the better and approve it, but I follow the worse."[22] Paul shows that often in life a person will do things he does not want to do and will not do things he very much wants to do.

That is normal! But God has a far better plan for the life of the believer. Praise God that He did not leave us to go through this life knowing only the defeat of never being able to overcome sin. Though Paul ended chapter seven with the contrast between the mind and the flesh, he begins chapter eight with some very exciting news.

> There is therefore now no condemnation for those who are in Christ Jesus. For the law of the Spirit of life in Christ Jesus has set you free from the law of sin and death. For what the Law could not do, weak as it was through the flesh, God *did*; sending His own Son in the likeness of sinful flesh and *as an offering* for sin, He condemned sin in the flesh, in order that the requirement of the Law might be fulfilled in us, who do not walk according to the flesh, but according to the Spirit. For those who are according to the flesh set their minds on the things of the flesh, but those who are according to the Spirit, the things of the Spirit. For the mind set on the flesh is death, but the mind set on the Spirit is life and peace, because the mind set on the flesh is hostile toward God; for it does not subject itself to the law of God, for it is not even able *to do so;* and those who are in the flesh cannot please God. However, you are not in the flesh but in the Spirit, if indeed the Spirit of God dwells in you. But if anyone does not have the Spirit of Christ, he does not belong to Him. And if Christ is in you, though the body is dead because of sin, yet the spirit is alive because of righteousness. But if the Spirit of Him who raised Jesus from the dead dwells in you, He who raised Christ Jesus from the dead will also give life to your mortal bodies through His Spirit who indwells you.
>
> So then, brethren, we are under obligation, not to the flesh, to live according to the flesh—for if you are living according to the flesh, you must die; but if by the Spirit you are putting to death the deeds of the body, you will live. For all who are being led by the Spirit of God, these are sons of God. For you have not received a spirit of slavery leading to fear again, but you have received a spirit of adoption as sons by which we cry out, "Abba! Father!" The Spirit Himself bears

witness with our spirit that we are children of God, and if children, heirs also, heirs of God and fellow heirs with Christ, if indeed we suffer with *Him* in order that we may also be glorified with *Him*. (Rom. 8:1–17 NASB)

Paul says, "There is no condemnation for those who are in Christ Jesus" (Rom. 8:1) and "Through Christ Jesus the law of the Spirit of life set me free from the law of sin and death" (Rom. 8:2). Who will set us free? Jesus! Even though we are weak and sinful, and we can't overcome sin by ourselves, Jesus came and "condemned sin in the flesh" (Rom. 8:3). The only one who was without sin (Heb. 4:15), died for our sins (I Cor. 15:3–4). Because Jesus fulfilled the requirements of the law, even though no one else could, we are no longer obligated to fulfill it. He did it for us. He did it for you.

Now the struggle shifts from Will I be able to fulfill the law? to Am I going to sow to the flesh or to the Spirit? That's a choice that each Christian has to answer. Paul wrote in Romans 8:6 that the mind that is set on the flesh produces death. That mindset is in direct opposition to God. It does not and cannot subject itself to the law of God. Andrew Murray says it is pointless to talk to carnal men about spiritual things. Here is his description of carnal men:

The carnal man:

1. He is prolonged in infancy.
2. Sin and failure have mastered him.
3. Carnality makes it impossible to receive spiritual truth.

How can a Christian go from being carnally minded to being spiritual?

1. He must first have faith and sight concerning the spiritual life.
2. He must be fully convinced that he is carnally minded.

3. He must believe that passing from carnal to spiritual mindedness takes place in only an instant. (Maturity does not but the decision does).
4. He must believe that Christ is able to keep him and he must always look to Christ to keep us.

The chief mark of the spiritual man is not that he has reached perfection, but that he is yielded to the Spirit of God.[23]

After Paul stated in Romans 8:6 that the mind set on the flesh is death, he said that the mind set on the Spirit is life and peace. The choice ultimately is this: does the person want death or life and peace?

The question that the believer needs to answer is this: Am I carnally minded or is my mind set on the Spirit?

The entire process of truly being wise about good and innocent about evil hinges on our mindset. Tomorrow we will look at how to change our thinking.

Food for thought:

- As Paul pointed out in Galatians chapter six, we either sow to the flesh or we sow to the Spirit in life. Constantly be striving to sow to the Spirit so that you will reap eternal life.
- Pray that God will help you to identify and remove anything that is remaining of the flesh and ask Him to help you to walk by the Spirit (Gal. 5:16, 25).

Day Eleven

Renew Your Mind

One ship drives east and another drives west
With the selfsame winds that blow.
'Tis the set of the sails
And not the gales which tells us the way to go.
Ella Wheeler Wilcox[24]

As we saw yesterday, there is a battle for your mind. It is our mindset that determines our direction in life. Charles Stanley, in his discussion of mindset talks about how mindset affects our lives. He describes the different mindsets that Jesus revealed in the parable of the soils (Matt. 13:1–9). He calls them a closed mind, a cloudy mind, a cluttered mind, and a committed mind.[25]

When a person finally comes to the realization that he does not have a committed mind, how does he make the changes necessary to become fully committed to following Christ?

Paul wrote to the church in Rome and had this to say:

> Therefore, I urge you, brothers, in view of God's mercy, to offer your bodies as living sacrifices, holy and pleasing to God—this is your spiritual act of worship. Do not conform any longer to the pattern of this world, but be transformed by the renewing of your mind. (Rom. 12:1–2)

Though many Christians may be content to live their lives with a carnal or fleshly mindset, this passage says that we should offer our bodies as living sacrifices. Throughout the Old Testament, if you study what sacrificial animals had to look forward to, you will find that their future was death. In other words, our spiritual act of worship begins with dying. Jesus said it this way: "If anyone would come after me, he must deny himself and take up his cross daily and follow me" (Luke 9:23). Denying ourselves and taking our cross to follow Christ means that we are daily saying, "Not my will but Yours be done."

The life of a living sacrifice should be holy and pleasing to God. In the next verse he discusses how we should be different from the world. We are to no longer conform to the world's pattern, but we are to be transformed. How? By renewing our minds!

How can we renew our minds? Paul addresses this question in a couple of different passages. 2 Corinthians 10:4–5 says, "The weapons we fight with are not the weapons of the world. On the contrary, they have divine power to demolish strongholds. We demolish arguments and every pretension that sets itself up against the knowledge of God, and we take captive every thought to make it obedient to Christ." Learn to take every thought captive and make it obedient to Christ.

Many public schools in America used to have signs posted in the cafeterias that read "You Are What You Eat." Lester Sumrall, in his book *Overcoming Compulsive Desires,* states that "there's no such thing as an idle thought. We are what we think."[26] Solomon said in Proverbs 23:7 (NASB) that it is how a man thinks in his heart that determines who he is.

Take every thought captive and make it obedient to Christ. Paul added more insight into how we do this when he wrote, "Finally, brothers, whatever is true, whatever is noble, whatever is right, whatever is pure, whatever is lovely, whatever is admirable—if anything is excellent or praiseworthy—think about such things" (Phil. 4:8). If it is true, noble, right, pure, lovely, admirable, excellent, or worthy of praise, let your mind dwell on it. If it is not one of these things, then don't dwell on it!

Thomas à Kempis said that a person should never relax his mind from attentive thought to heavenly things. What a person puts into his mind is what he will get out of it. In the computer world there is a phrase that is commonly used: GIGO or "garbage in, garbage out." Jesus said that it is what fills the heart that will determine what a person says. And it is what comes out of the heart that makes a person clean or unclean (Matt. 15:17–20).

Return to Innocence

In his book *The Glorious Journey*, Charles Stanley graphically portrays how radically different the follower of Christ should think than people in the world. In fact, he points out that the remedy for worldliness is a renewed mind.

World's Lie	God's Truth	
Everything revolves around you.	You are part of the Lord's body.	(Romans 12:5)
Get me and I'll get even.	Leave vengeance to God.	(Romans 12:19)
Love is always conditional.	Love others anyway.	(Romans 13:8)
My view is the right view.	Accept others without judging.	(Romans 14:1)
Don't get involved.	Get involved.	(Romans 15:1-6)
Only hang around people just like you.	Accept others just like Jesus accepted you.	(Romans 14:7-13)[27]

If our goal is to renew our thinking so that we can return to innocence, we have to start by changing the things that are entering our minds. If we fill our minds with garbage, then that is what we will get back; and if we fill our minds with those things that are pure and right and noble, as Philippians 4:8 teaches, then those are the things we will get back. Generally speaking, this is also an area that we have almost total control over. Though certainly some things are placed in front of us through no fault of ours, there are many more things that we allow to enter our minds by the choices we make. For example, the television shows we watch, the movies we see, the books and magazines we read, etc., are things that we control. Tomorrow we will take some time to start examining just how we can actively start changing what enters our minds.

Food for thought:

- We are told in Corinthians that we should take every thought captive to make it obedient to Christ (2 Cor. 10:5). Paul told the church in Rome that we should be transformed by renewing our minds (Rom. 12:1–2).
- When you find yourself thinking about something that is ungodly, deliberately change what you are *dwelling* on. Replace what you're thinking about with things that will draw you closer to the Lord.
- Pray that God will help you to cultivate the mind of Christ.

Day Twelve

Guard Your Eyes and Ears

> Your eye is the lamp of your body. When your eyes are good, your whole body also is full of light. But when they are bad, your body also is full of darkness. See to it, then, that the light within you is not darkness. Therefore, if your whole body is full of light, and no part of it dark, it will be completely lighted, as when the light of a lamp shines on you. (Luke 11:34–36)

It is time to get really practical. Jesus said that what we look at will determine whether we are filled with light or darkness. As was stated yesterday, this is something that we control. We determine whether darkness will enter us by whether or not we allow ourselves to look at things that will fill us with darkness. This can be applied to what a person watches on television, what movies he watches, or what books or magazines he reads. It will affect how he looks at other people and virtually every area of his life. Job applied this principle to himself in this way: "I made a covenant with my eyes not to look lustfully at a girl" (Job 31:1). Rather than allowing darkness (or sin) to enter through our eyes, Christians should commit to making sure that we only allow light to enter.

Someone might argue that only looking is not a problem, but Jesus said this: "Anyone who looks at a woman lustfully has already committed adultery with her in his heart" (Matt. 5:28).

We need to always keep in mind that all through the Sermon on the Mount Jesus keeps coming back to the concept that God is looking at our hearts. Even though a person may not have committed the physical act of adultery, if he has committed the act in his heart then he is just as guilty of sin. This makes the idea of guarding our eyes even more imperative.

So, how do we fill our eyes with light? Psalm 119:105 says, "Your word is a lamp to my feet and a light for my path." We will spend more time dealing with this concept in a later chapter, but one very important activity that will allow light to enter our eyes and our souls is feeding daily on the Word of God.

We can begin changing the way that we think by changing what we allow to come in through our eyes, but we can also help to change the way that we think by changing what we allow to come in through our ears. Some congregations still sing a children's song that says "Be careful little ears what you hear." This is excellent advice! In fact, Jesus said that people should consider carefully what they hear (Mark 4:24).

Earlier reference was made to the computer term GIGO, or garbage in, garbage out. We also looked at Paul's statements concerning the necessity to renew our minds (Rom. 12:1–2). A good beginning point in renewing our minds—and that's all this is so far, a beginning—is to change what we allow to come in through our eyes and our ears.

So what is it that would make some Christians decide to take these things to heart and others not give them a second thought? It is what Andrew Murray called "absolute surrender."[28] To truly change the way we think, we must be totally committed to following Christ. That total commitment is what we will discuss tomorrow.

Food for thought:

- A children's song says, "Be careful little eyes what you see." We need to cultivate the habit of guarding our eyes and ears.
- Spend some time thinking about what you allow your eyes to dwell on. Do those things help you to grow stronger in your faith? Do they help you to become a more Christ-like person? Ask the same questions about the things that you listen to.
- Jesus said the your eyes are the lamp of you body. Don't allow things in that will contaminate your mind. Guard you eyes and ears carefully.

Day Thirteen

Absolute Surrender

In 1875 Hannah Whitall Smith wrote,

> The standard of practical holy living has been so low among Christians that very often the person who tries to practice spiritual disciplines in everyday life is looked upon with disapproval by a large portion of the church. And for the most part, the followers of Jesus Christ are satisfied with a life so conformed to the world, and so like it in almost every respect, that to a casual observer there is no difference between the Christian and the pagan.[29]

If we want God's blessing on our lives, we must realize that He calls for absolute surrender. There are two sides to absolute surrender: one, doing what God wants us to do, and two, letting God do whatever He wants to do in our lives. Surrender means transferring ownership.[30]

Now let's look at what the Scriptures say on this issue. As we saw in Romans 12:1 we are to offer ourselves as living sacrifices. We need to take time here to look at the subject of dying in the Bible. "So then, brethren, we are under obligation, not to the flesh, to live according to the flesh—for if you are living according to the flesh, you must die; but if by the Spirit you are putting to death the deeds of the body, you will live" (Rom. 8:12–13). The phrase "if by the Spirit you are putting to death the deeds of the body" indicates an ongoing process. (We will look at this process more in a later chapter.)

Several passages in the New Testament say that God has called us to die. Apparently some have taken the doctrine of grace and have tried to use it as a license to sin. This seems to be the problem that Paul was addressing when he wrote the following words:

What shall we say, then? Shall we go on sinning so that grace may increase? By no means! We died to sin; how can we live in it any longer? Or don't you know that all of us who were baptized into Christ Jesus were baptized into his death? We were therefore buried with him through baptism into death in order that, just as Christ was raised from the dead through the glory of the Father, we too may live a new life.

If we have been united with him like this in his death, we will certainly also be united with him in his resurrection. For we know that our old self was crucified with him so that the body of sin might be done away with, that we should no longer be slaves to sin—because anyone who has died has been freed from sin.

Now if we died with Christ, we believe that we will also live with him. For we know that since Christ was raised from the dead, he cannot die again; death no longer has mastery over him. The death he died, he died to sin once for all; but the life he lives, he lives to God.

In the same way, count yourselves dead to sin but alive to God in Christ Jesus. Therefore do not let sin reign in your mortal body so that you obey its evil desires. Do not offer the parts of your body to sin, as instruments of wickedness, but rather offer yourselves to God, as those who have been brought from death to life; and offer the parts of your body to him as instruments of righteousness. For sin shall not be your master, because you are not under law, but under grace. (Rom. 6:1–14)

In verse two Paul said that we died to sin. In verse six he said that we had been crucified with Christ so that the body of sin might be done away with. Verse seven says that anyone who has died has been freed from sin. Verse eleven says we should count ourselves as dead to sin. Verse twelve tells us not to let sin reign in our bodies. And verse thirteen states that we can choose between offering our bodies as instruments of wickedness or righteousness. All of these verses discuss the concept of dying to sin.

In Galatians 2:20 Paul said, "I have been crucified with Christ and I no longer live, but Christ lives in me. The life I live in the body, I live by faith in the Son of God, who loved me and gave himself for me." He went on to say, "Those who belong to Christ Jesus have crucified the flesh with its passions and desires" (Gal. 5:24). In the next verse he said, "If we live by the Spirit, let us also walk by the Spirit." This introduces another subject that is a vital key to becoming wise about good and innocent about evil, namely, the role of the Holy Spirit. We will examine that role more tomorrow.

Paul's desire was never to boast "except in the cross of our Lord Jesus Christ, through which the world has been crucified to me, and I to the world" (Gal. 6:14).

John describes this world, or worldliness, as including the lust of the flesh, the lust of the eyes, and the pride of life (1 John 2:16–17).

Jesus said that a disciple should count the cost to see if he really wanted to be His follower. Listen to this passage: "If anyone comes to me and does not hate his father and mother, his wife and children, his brothers and sisters—yes, even his own life—he cannot be my disciple. And anyone who does not carry his cross and follow me cannot be my disciple" (Luke 14:26–27). He also stated in Matthew 6:24 that "no one can serve two masters."

These passages lead us to one conclusion: Jesus accepts nothing less than absolute surrender. He calls us to die to self, to sin, to the law, and to the world. And He desires for us to dedicate our entire life to His service. Just as Jesus prayed in the garden, "not my will, but yours be done" (Luke 22:42), God demands that we surrender ourselves to Him this same way.

Christians have not been called to live a life that will indulge the flesh. No, we have been called to die to the flesh. But the part that we have not really looked at today is that we cannot live this kind of life based on our own strength or righteousness. As Paul revealed in Galatians 3:4, it is not by human effort. The truly good news is that God does not expect us to achieve it on our own. Tomorrow we will look at the role our Comforter plays in enabling us to live the life that God has called us to.

Food for thought:

- It's time for more soul searching. Is there *anything* in your life that is not in submission to God? Another way of asking this: Is there anything that is more important to you than your relationship with God?
- If you find anything in your life that has been more important to you than your relationship with the Lord, repent. God will not take second place.
- Spend time in prayer seeking direction concerning where you are and where you need to be. God has promised that if we draw near to Him, He will draw near to us (James 4:8). How close you are to God is up to you.

Sowing to the Spirit

Day Fourteen

The Role of the Spirit

If by the Spirit you put to death the misdeeds of the body, you will live (Rom. 8:13). Today we will examine the concept of what the Spirit does in the believer's life and how He helps us to put to death the misdeeds spoken of above.

The truth is that without God's provision in this area we can never be pure. If we are living by the Spirit, we will not gratify the desires of the flesh (Gal. 5:16). If we are *not* living by the Spirit we will continue to gratify those desires. If we take a closer look at the context in which this statement was made, we will see that Paul was discussing the contrast between the flesh and the Spirit. "The acts of the flesh are obvious: sexual immorality, impurity and debauchery; idolatry and witchcraft; hatred, discord, jealousy, fits of rage, selfish ambition, dissensions, factions and envy; drunkenness, orgies, and the like" (Gal. 5:19). In contrast, the fruit of the Spirit is "love, joy, peace, patience, kindness, goodness, faithfulness, gentleness and self-control" (Gal. 5:22–23).

There is a huge difference between fleshly living and the fruit that the Spirit produces. God wants His followers to be people who are filled with the fruit of the Spirit.

What are some of the things that the Spirit actually does in the life of believers to help them in their walks with God? According to Romans 2:28–29, He circumcises the heart. We learn in Romans 5:5 that the Spirit pours God's love into our hearts. 1 Corinthians 2:12 tells us that the Spirit enables us to understand what God has freely given to us. (In other words, if we do not have the Spirit then we cannot understand those things.) The Spirit strengthens the believer with power in the inner man (Eph. 3:16). The Spirit leads us (Gal. 5:18). In fact, Paul wrote that it is "those who are led by the Spirit of God" who are "Sons of God" (Rom. 8:18). Another part of His ministry is to transform us to the likeness of Christ (2 Cor. 3:18). The Spirit sanctifies the believer (1 Peter 1:2, Rom. 15:16,2; Thess. 2:13). And, finally, we should keep ourselves pure from sexual sin because our body is the temple of the Spirit who dwells in us (1 Cor. 6:18–20).

If we carefully examine each of the things listed above, we will quickly realize how utterly futile it would be for anyone to try to do these things based on his own strength. God is the one who enables us to be spiritual by placing His Spirit within us and allowing His Spirit to transform us to be like Jesus.

The hard part of this whole topic is trying to maintain a proper balance. On one hand, we have the responsibility to obey God, and we need to work hard to make sure we are obedient in all that He has commanded us. On the other hand, we see from Scripture that we are completely incapable of being spiritual because we are fleshly beings. But God has provided us with His Spirit to see us through that dilemma. Some may say that there is nothing that we can do because God does everything; so we don't have any responsibilities. Yet we see from Scripture that God does require our obedience. So how do we get these apparent contradictions to mesh?

This answer may be an over simplification, but since we will spend most of the rest of this book expanding on it, it should suffice for now. God knows that without His help we aren't capable of being spiritual people. So He has provided "everything we need for life and godliness" (2 Pet. 1:3). God also expects us to "work out our salvation with fear and trembling" (Phil. 2:12). While Paul is not teaching that works will save us (Eph. 2:9), he is telling us that to be pleasing to God we are required to work. James said it this way:

But someone will say, "You have faith; I have deeds."

Show me your faith without deeds, and I will show you my faith by what I do. You believe that there is one God. Good! Even the demons believe that and shudder.

You foolish man, do you want evidence that faith without deeds is useless? Was not our ancestor Abraham considered righteous for what he did when he offered his son Isaac on the altar? You see that his faith and his actions were working together, and his faith was made complete by what he did. And the scripture was fulfilled that says, "Abraham believed God, and it was credited to him as righteousness," and he was called God's friend. You see that a person is justified by what he does and not by faith alone.

In the same way, was not Rahab the prostitute considered righteous for what she did when she gave lodging to the spies and sent them off in a different direction? As the body without the spirit is dead, so faith without deeds is dead. (James 2:18–26)

Paul and James are not disagreeing with one another. Paul says that works will not save you. James says that a true believer will work because he is saved. We are not studying these things that help us grow wise about good and innocent about evil because we are trying to earn our salvation. God has already taken care of that by extending His grace to us and covering us with the precious blood of Jesus. We are studying this because John told us in 1 John 3:2–3 that everyone who has the hope of seeing Jesus as He is and being made like Him will purify himself. This purification process takes work. But the exciting thing is that God has not left us alone to make all of these changes. His Spirit is dwelling within us and is working to transform us to be like Christ (2 Cor. 3:18). God has truly given us "everything we need for life and godliness" (2 Peter 1:3).

Food for thought:

- Paul asked the Christians in Galatia, "After beginning with the Spirit, are you now trying to attain your goal by human effort?" (Gal. 3:3). For us to become genuinely spiritual people we have to realize that we can't do it based on human effort or human reasoning. Apart from the work of the Spirit in us, we are incapable of producing spirituality.
- Ask the Lord to help you to give Him the control that He needs in order to produce within you the changes that He desires to make.

DAY FIFTEEN

The Fruit of the Spirit Is Love

> But the fruit of the Spirit is love, joy, peace, patience, kindness, goodness, faithfulness, gentleness and self-control. Against such things there is no law. (Gal. 5:22–24)

Those who belong to Christ Jesus have crucified the sinful nature with its passions and desires.

As we examine this text, we will look at each area of our lives that the Lord desperately wants to transform. The first area where God wants to shine in our lives is in *love*. The fruit of the Spirit is love. Before we take the time to look at some biblical references to love, let me ask you this question: Are you currently living a life known by love?

The reason I start this discussion with a question like that is that I do not want you to simply gloss over the upcoming material and say, "Been there, done that." I want you to realize that these are truths that God views as critical to your development. Please do not take them lightly.

Jesus was asked one day what the greatest commandment might be.

> "The most important one," answered Jesus, "is this: 'Hear, O Israel, the Lord our God, the Lord is one. Love the Lord your God with all your heart and with all your soul and with all your mind and with all your strength.' The second is this: 'Love your neighbor as yourself.' There is no commandment greater than these." (Mark 12:28–31)

Love God with all you heart, with all your soul, with all your mind, and with all your strength. Love Him with every fiber of your being. Fall in love with Him. Love Him with your intellect, with your passions, with your time, with your money, with your job, with everything. Why is it that so many times we allow ourselves to love God with our leftovers? If we have any time left over, we will give it to God. If we have any money left over, we will give that to Him. Jesus tells us here and throughout His ministry that God will not and should not have to play second fiddle. God should be the number one priority in you life—period. If you are not currently in love with God, start working on cultivating a passion for Him. Ask Him to show you what areas of your life are coming between you and Him and how you need to change.

The Lord went on to say that the second command is much like the first and it is to love your neighbor as you love yourself. First of all, He assumed that you would love yourself. This is not talking about being self-centered or selfish. But He is saying that a healthy self-image and good self-esteem are important if we are to be able to show genuine love to other people. If you don't love or care about yourself, you cannot possibly show meaningful love to anyone else.

Let's examine some of what we learn from scripture about living a life of love.

> It was just before the Passover Feast. Jesus knew that the time had come for him to leave this world and go to the Father. Having loved his own who were in the world, he now showed them the full extent of his love.
>
> The evening meal was being served, and the devil had already prompted Judas Iscariot, son of Simon, to betray Jesus. Jesus knew that the Father had put all things under his power, and that he had come from God and was returning to God; so he got up from the meal, took off his outer clothing, and wrapped a towel around his waist. After that, he poured water into a basin and began to wash his disciples' feet, drying them with the towel that was wrapped around him. (John 13:1–5)

Jesus knows that He is getting ready to die. It is His last night with the disciples, and He wants to show them the full extent of His love. So what does He do? Does He go into a long discourse on how He loved them enough to leave heaven and to go to the cross for them? No! He gets down on His hands and knees and begins to wash the filth off their feet. Not just the feet of James and John, but also the feet of Judas. Even though He knew that Judas was getting ready to betray Him, Jesus still washed his feet. The message Jesus wants to be sure we get is to start demonstrating His love to others. Wow!

Later, in John 13:34–35, Jesus said that the world would recognize true disciples by this one thing: they'll love each other. This love is not talking about the warm or fuzzy feeling we get when we are "in love" with that someone special. Biblical love is a decision to treat the other person and his or her needs as an important priority. Let's look at how Paul defines genuine love in 1 Corinthians chapter 13:

> Love is patient, love is kind. It does not envy, it does not boast, it is not proud. It is not rude, it is not self-seeking, it is not easily angered, it keeps no record of wrongs. Love does not delight in evil but rejoices with the truth. It always protects, always trusts, always hopes, always perseveres. Love never fails. (1 Cor. 13:4–8)

Patient, kind, no envy, no boasting, no pride, no rudeness, no seeking of self, not easily angered, keeping no records of wrongs, not delighting in evil, but rejoicing with the truth, protecting, trusting, hoping, persevering, never failing. What a powerful definition of what real love is and is not. It is treating people with respect. It is showing them not just with words, but also with actions, that they have value. It says, "You matter. I'm not going to look at how often you've blown it, but I'm going to look for ways to lift you up and will always strive to make your life a little bit better." Love says, "Even if it means I need to get down on my hands and knees and try to get the dirt out from between your toes, that's what I'll do." That's what Jesus did.

The beautiful part of what God does is that He doesn't simply say, "Love others." He demonstrated love for us and then He goes out of His way to equip us to live the lifestyle He calls us to. In John 3:16 we're told that God loved the world (you and me) so much that He gave His only son to die for us. He loved so much that He gave. We demonstrate our love (or lack of love) by what we are or are not willing to give. Are we willing to give our time? Our money? Our talents? Our reputations? Love gives! Selfishness takes.

Let's look at Romans five.

> Therefore, since we have been justified through faith, we have peace with God through our Lord Jesus Christ, through whom we have gained access by faith into this grace in which we now stand. And we rejoice in the hope of the glory of God. Not only so, but we also rejoice in our sufferings, because we know that suffering produces perseverance; perseverance, character; and character, hope. And hope does not disappoint us, because God has poured out his love into our hearts by the Holy Spirit, whom he has given us. (Rom. 5:1–5)

God has poured His love into your heart by the Holy Spirit. What a wonderful gift! Not only has God commanded us to love, but He has equipped us to do it as well. In Galatians five we're told that the fruit the Spirit produces within us is love. So, if we are not living authentically loving lives, the blame is not with God. We are doing something that is hindering Him from getting through. It may be an unwillingness to forgive someone. It may be resentment. It may be that we're harboring hatred or some kind of animosity toward someone. But when we are keeping records of wrongs suffered, when we are holding on to grudges, we are not demonstrating real love.

The greatest commandments are to "love the Lord your God with all your heart, and with all your soul, and with all your mind, and with all your strength," and to "love your neighbor as you love yourself (Mark 12:28–31). Don't settle for anything less.

Food for thought:

- Are there things in your life that are more important to you than your relationship with God?
- Are there people with whom you need to mend broken relationships?
- Spend some time in prayer asking the Lord to show you how to make love a priority in your life. Ask Him to show you those areas where you need to improve and to reveal to you how you can make the necessary changes.
- Remember, it is by the love Christians show one for another that the world will recognize genuine believers. Let them see Christ living in you. Dare to put on a towel and wash some feet if that's what is required.

Day Sixteen

The Fruit of the Spirit Is Joy

"The fruit of the Spirit is . . . joy" (Gal. 5:22). Have you ever wondered how it could be that Paul and Silas could be sitting in jail singing praises to God? (Acts 16:25). It certainly was not because they were so thrilled with their surroundings that they just had to burst into song. They were not saying that the food was great and the air conditioning was so comfortable that they just felt like singing. Remember, they were in jail. They had been arrested for preaching the gospel. Yet they were praising God. They had a joy that comes only from a close communion with God. This demonstrates the power of passages like Psalm 16:11, which says "You fill me with joy in your presence." Isn't it amazing that the presence of God can be felt even in a jail cell?

Real joy is not dependent upon circumstances. Authentic joy comes through relationship. It is fruit that the Spirit produces in our lives when we allow Him to lead us and transform us.

As we examine the fruit of the Spirit it is interesting to note that in each area, we have the fruit that He produces and we have our responsibility of sowing to Him as well. The Spirit is not going to waste His time trying to force us to become something we are unwilling to become. It amazes me to see how many times we come across people who profess to be Christians and yet when you talk to them they act like they were weaned on prune juice when they were growing up. You'd think that if they ever smiled it would destroy their face. Yet an intimate walk with God produces a joy that bubbles over into every area of our lives (including our faces).

Romans 14:17 says, "For the kingdom of God is not a matter of eating and drinking, but of righteousness, peace and joy in the Holy Spirit." If the kingdom of God is a matter of joy, why do so many believers seem to have so little of it in their lives? I believe that at least part of the answer is that many who wear the name of Christ are still living their lives based on their own strength and understanding instead of fully surrendering to Him. Wonderful changes begin to take place when we acknowledge how much we need the Lord and we open our hearts and minds to Him and say to the Potter, "I'm available for You to transform into whatever You want me to be." Oh, the magnificent joy of living in His presence.

"Enter his gates with thanksgiving and his courts with praise" (Ps. 100:4). If you want to enter into the King's gate, the required password is to give thanks. But if you want to get into the inner court where the King is seated on His throne, you need to learn to give praise. This is why Paul and Silas could sing praises at midnight. They were going into the presence of God regardless of their surroundings. We can do the same. In fact, we are commanded to at least have the same outlook. Look at 1 Thessalonians 5:16–18: "Be joyful always; pray continually; give thanks in all circumstances, for this is God's will for you in Christ Jesus." That doesn't say that you need to try to be happy when life is going great, but when circumstances are rather bleak it's all right to miserable and grumpy. It says that whatever circumstances you face, you need to be joyful and give thanks. That is God's will for your life! No, that doesn't come naturally. Yes, it requires a lot of work and a lot of faith. But, as we allow the Spirit to bear fruit in our lives, the joy will increase and our ability to respond to adversity with joy will improve.

Food for thought:

- Are you able to rejoice when it seems there is nothing happening in your life to be happy about?
- Spend some time in prayer asking God to show you whether or not there are things in your life that are keeping you from experiencing the joy of His presence. Is there ongoing sin? Are there damaged relationships?
- God wants you to rejoice and give thanks in all circumstances. What situation are you facing right now that you haven't thanked God in? When we thank Him, even in circumstances that we don't like or understand, we step out in faith and He is glorified in spite of the situation that we face.

Day Seventeen

The Fruit of the Spirit Is Peace

Does it ever bother you to look around and see so many people with absolutely no peace in their lives? People are struggling with marriage problems; some are having problems with their kids or their parents; some are facing battles with alcohol, drugs, porn, or other forms of sexual immorality. It seems as though the story of many people's lives would be turmoil. Yet the fruit the Spirit produces is peace. Paul said in Galatians 6:7 that we will reap what we sow. If we sow to the flesh, we will reap destruction; and if we sow to the Spirit, we will reap eternal life. We choose!

Let's examine the fruit that God wants to produce: peace. "For to us a child is born, to us a son is given, and the government will be on his shoulders. And he will be called Wonderful Counselor, Mighty God, Everlasting Father, Prince of Peace" (Isa. 9:6). Jesus is called the Prince of Peace. He is the master of providing peace to those whose lives have been lacking it. Romans 14:17 says that the kingdom of God is a matter of peace. What does that mean to our daily lives? It means that when our enemy tries to disrupt our lives, we need to realize that confusion, fear, turmoil, hatred, animosity, discord, etc., are all things that he brings. He is a liar and a murderer (John 8:44). Examine the fruit to see whether or not something is from God. The Prince of Peace brings peace, joy, and stability to life. He offers hope. But to see that and live it we have to be willing to surrender every part of our lives to His Lordship.

Ephesians 6:15 talks about "the gospel of peace." We will examine this in a lot more detail on day 36, but today I'd like to point out that the good news that Jesus offers to people's lives includes the peace that only He can provide. Yes, he knows how much you are hurting. He knows everything there is to know about your struggles and He still offers peace and comfort. In fact God is called the "God of all comfort" in 2 Corinthians 1:3.

Let's look at Philippians 4:6–7

> Do not be anxious about anything, but in everything, by prayer and petition, with thanksgiving, present your requests to God. And the peace of God, which transcends all understanding, will guard your hearts and your minds in Christ Jesus.

Don't be anxious about anything? When life seems to be falling apart, worry doesn't help. The desired response is to pray. Give thanks, and tell God what's on your heart. His response is to provide a peace that can't be expressed in human words. He will guard both your heart and your mind in Christ Jesus.

So why are so many Christians struggling with worry and doubt? Because most of us don't listen to the first part of this passage. Our natural tendency seems to be to worry and fret and, oh yeah, when all else fails, try prayer. Peter told us in 1 Peter 5:7 to cast *all* our anxiety on Him because He cares for us. Please listen to what he says. God cares about your life! When you are hurting, He cares! When you are struggling with fear or doubt, He cares! No matter how big or seemingly insignificant your pain may be, He cares! Cast your anxiety on Him. He can handle it. He wants to fill your life with peace. But He can do that only when you fill your life with Him.

Food for thought:

- Are there any circumstances in your life in which you are unable or unwilling to give thanks?
- Are there anxieties that you have been unwilling to let go of?
- Spend some time soul searching and asking God to shine the light of truth on every aspect of your life so that you can genuinely let go and allow Him to fill your life with the "peace that passes understanding."

Day Eighteen

The Fruit of the Spirit Is Patience

And we pray this in order that you may live a life worthy of the Lord and may please him in every way: bearing fruit in every good work, growing in the knowledge of God, being strengthened with all power according to his glorious might so that you may have great endurance and patience, and joyfully giving thanks to the Father, who has qualified you to share in the inheritance of the saints in the kingdom of light. For he has rescued us from the dominion of darkness and brought us into the kingdom of the Son he loves, in whom we have redemption, the forgiveness of sins. (Col. 1:10–14)

Therefore, as God's chosen people, holy and dearly loved, clothe yourselves with compassion, kindness, humility, gentleness and patience. (Col. 3:12)

We pray that you will live *a life worthy of the Lord*. Bear fruit. Grow in the knowledge of God. As you are strengthened with power according to God's glorious might, endurance and patience will grow. It is during the times in life when we recognize that circumstances are beyond our control that we can turn to the Lord and allow Him to equip us with ever-increasing endurance and patience; so Paul told the church at Colossae to clothe themselves with patience.

Living a life worthy of the Lord is really what much of this book is about. As we begin to learn what it means to be wise about what is good and innocent about what is evil, we start learning more of what it means to emulate Christ. We will later examine the process of how patience is often produced in our lives, but in order to really attain the patience or perseverance that God wants to produce within us we have to stop short-circuiting the process. Our natural tendency is to run from any form of adversity. Just as the children of Israel did when the Lord sent poisonous snakes into the camp (Num. 21). Their natural response was to beg the Lord to remove the snakes. God had a different plan: to leave the snakes and provide a way for them to survive if they were bitten. Very often in our lives, rather than simply removing every difficult situation that we face, He allows the struggles to continue so that we can mature.

> Brothers, as an example of patience in the face of suffering, take the prophets who spoke in the name of the Lord. As you know, we consider blessed those who have persevered. You have heard of Job's perseverance and have seen what the Lord finally brought about. The Lord is full of compassion and mercy. (James 5:10–11)

Let's look at Job's situation.

> In the land of Uz there lived a man whose name was Job. This man was blameless and upright; he feared God and shunned evil. He had seven sons and three daughters, and he owned seven thousand sheep, three thousand camels, five hundred yoke of oxen and five hundred donkeys, and had a large number of servants. He was the greatest man among all the people of the East. . . . One day the angels came to present themselves before the LORD, and Satan also came with them. The LORD said to Satan, "Where have you come from?"
>
> Satan answered the LORD, "From roaming through the earth and going back and forth in it."
>
> Then the LORD said to Satan, "Have you considered my servant Job? There is no one on earth like him; he is blameless and upright, a man who fears God and shuns evil."
>
> "Does Job fear God for nothing?" Satan replied. "Have you not put a hedge around him and his household and everything he has? You have blessed the work of his hands, so that his flocks and herds are spread throughout the land. But stretch out your hand and strike everything he has, and he will surely curse you to your face."

Sowing to the Spirit

The LORD said to Satan, "Very well, then, everything he has is in your hands, but on the man himself do not lay a finger."

Then Satan went out from the presence of the LORD.

One day when Job's sons and daughters were feasting and drinking wine at the oldest brother's house, a messenger came to Job and said, "The oxen were plowing and the donkeys were grazing nearby, and the Sabeans attacked and carried them off. They put the servants to the sword, and I am the only one who has escaped to tell you!"

While he was still speaking, another messenger came and said, "The fire of God fell from the sky and burned up the sheep and the servants, and I am the only one who has escaped to tell you!"

While he was still speaking, another messenger came and said, "The Chaldeans formed three raiding parties and swept down on your camels and carried them off. They put the servants to the sword, and I am the only one who has escaped to tell you!"

While he was still speaking, yet another messenger came and said, "Your sons and daughters were feasting and drinking wine at the oldest brother's house, when suddenly a mighty wind swept in from the desert and struck the four corners of the house. It collapsed on them and they are dead, and I am the only one who has escaped to tell you!"

At this, Job got up and tore his robe and shaved his head. Then he fell to the ground in worship and said:

"Naked I came from my mother's womb, and naked I will depart.

The LORD gave and the LORD has taken away; may the name of the LORD be praised."

In all this, Job did not sin by charging God with wrongdoing. (Job 1:1–22)

In one day Job lost virtually everything he had—all ten of his children. all his household servants, all his wealth. Gone. Yet Job continued to give God praise. But the struggles got worse.

On another day the angels came to present themselves before the LORD, and Satan also came with them to present himself before him. And the LORD said to Satan, "Where have you come from?"

Satan answered the LORD, "From roaming through the earth and going back and forth in it."

Then the LORD said to Satan, "Have you considered my servant Job? There is no one on earth like him; he is blameless and upright, a man who fears God and shuns evil. And he still maintains his integrity, though you incited me against him to ruin him without any reason."

"Skin for skin!" Satan replied. "A man will give all he has for his own life. But stretch out your hand and strike his flesh and bones, and he will surely curse you to your face."

The LORD said to Satan, "Very well, then, he is in your hands; but you must spare his life."

So Satan went out from the presence of the LORD and afflicted Job with painful sores from the soles of his feet to the top of his head. Then Job took a piece of broken pottery and scraped himself with it as he sat among the ashes.

His wife said to him, "Are you still holding on to your integrity? Curse God and die!"

He replied, "You are talking like a foolish woman. Shall we accept good from God, and not trouble?"

In all this, Job did not sin in what he said. (Job 2:1–10)

Now Satan had actually touched Job's physical body, yet Job did not sin with his mouth. Soon after this some of Job's "friends" showed up to comfort him. For seven days they simply sat with him. They probably did provide some measure of comfort until they opened their mouths and blew it. Much of the rest of the book of Job deals with his friends and their faulty assumptions. I believe there are many times today when people can fall into the same misguided assumptions that Job's friends did. When we see someone struggling, very often people assume that it is because of some sin in their lives. Then we may begin to offer advice based on what has been assumed. Job's friends were condemned by God for what they falsely accused Job of doing. At times people do struggle because of sin in their lives and that does need to be addressed, but there are other times when things going wrong may be a test, or they may be for God's glory in another area of our lives. We cannot presume to know ultimately what God has in mind. We need to learn that God is glorified when we are willing to face every situation with faith, thanksgiving, and praise. In fact, Paul told the church in Thessalonica that it is God's will for us to give thanks in all circumstances (1 Thess. 5:18).

So, let's look at the process.

Therefore, since we have been justified through faith, we have peace with God through our Lord Jesus Christ, through whom we have gained access by faith into this grace in which we now stand. And we rejoice in the hope of the glory of God. Not only so, but we also rejoice in our sufferings, because we know that suffering produces perseverance; perseverance, character; and character, hope. And hope does not disappoint us, because God has poured out his love into our hearts by the Holy Spirit, whom he has given us. (Rom. 5:1–5)

We rejoice in our sufferings because suffering produces perseverance. Perseverance produces character, and character produces hope. Yes, it's a painful process at times, but it's the only way we can mature. Rejoicing in suffering is not talking about enjoying the pain. It is a decision and a deliberate act of faith that says, "Even though I don't like what I'm facing, I choose to believe that God can and will handle this and that He spoke the truth when He said that He causes all things to 'work together for good to those who love Him and are called according to His purpose' (Rom. 8:28). Father, thank You for the good You are going to produce through this struggle."

Consider it pure joy, my brothers, whenever you face trials of many kinds, because you know that the testing of your faith develops perseverance. Perseverance must finish its work so that you may be mature and complete, not lacking anything. (James 1:2–4)

Patience has to complete its work within us if we are to be mature Christians. So the tests will come. We are to "consider it pure joy" because when our faith is tested, perseverance is being developed and we are growing toward maturity.

"The fruit of the Spirit is . . . patience" (Gal. 5:22). God wants to produce patience in your life, but He can't complete His work if you are constantly running from the process. Learn to recognize the process. Commit to responding in faith and trust God to genuinely do what is in your best interest. He loves you so much more than you can possibly understand; let Him produce His masterpiece in you. Consider it pure joy when you encounter various trials—remembering that God is still working on your life.

Food for thought:

- Look back over your life and think about all the struggles you've already faced. Have you ever taken the time to thank God for what He was producing through them? Please do.
- Please take the time to recognize that deciding to consider it pure joy when we encounter trials is an act of faith. God is glorified when we deliberately choose to respond in faith to the circumstances of life. Let Him produce His complete work in you.

Day Nineteen

The Fruit of the Spirit Is Kindness

> And the Lord's servant must not quarrel; instead, he must be kind to everyone, able to teach, not resentful. Those who oppose him he must gently instruct, in the hope that God will grant them repentance leading them to a knowledge of the truth, and that they will come to their senses and escape from the trap of the devil, who has taken them captive to do his will. (2 Tim. 2:24–26)

The Lord's servant must be kind to everyone. How often have we seen people who were unkind or harsh in the name of defending the truth (or been guilty of it ourselves)? There is a radical difference between "gently instructing" (vs. 25) those with whom we have differences and the legalistic and often cruel attacks that frequently come from people who may think a little too highly of their own spirituality. "Kind to everyone." What a lofty goal. Kind to your spouse, kind to your children or parents. Kind to your boss or your employees. Kind to that person who acts like he would love nothing better than to be assured that your day was going to be miserable. Kind to everyone. The reason for having this as our goal is to help save souls. Live so you can keep the doors open for the gospel to spread.

> Do not let any unwholesome talk come out of your mouths, but only what is helpful for building others up according to their needs, that it may benefit those who listen. And do not grieve the Holy Spirit of God, with whom you were sealed for the day of redemption. Get rid of all bitterness, rage and anger, brawling and slander, along with every form of malice. Be kind and compassionate to one another, forgiving each other, just as in Christ God forgave you. (Eph. 4:29–32)

Several things in this passage are worthy of note. First of all, Paul says that our goal should be to never allow anything unwholesome to come out of our mouths. That means if you have to say "excuse my French" or "excuse my language"—don't say it. If you're tempted to tell a crude joke—don't! Second, our aim is to be sure that whatever does pass our lips will benefit the ones who hear our words. In verse thirty-two we see three more areas that need to be priorities in our daily lives: kindness, compassion, and forgiveness. Be kind to one another. Be compassionate and forgive each other, the same way you have been forgiven in Christ. Incidentally, forgiving others is not optional in Christ. "And when you stand praying, if you hold anything against anyone, forgive him, so that your Father in heaven may forgive you your sins" (Mark 11:25). If you hold *anything* against *anyone*. That doesn't leave anyone out. I can hear some of you saying, "But you don't know what this person has done to me." That's not the point! Think back to the cross. While Jesus was being murdered, His cry to His Father was, "Forgive them" (Luke 23:34). The rest of Mark eleven says that if you are unwilling to forgive, the Father can't forgive you. Forgiving is not optional. Yes, I know it's hard to forgive some people for some of the terrible things they have done, but God can help you here. Let it go.

> Therefore, as God's chosen people, holy and dearly loved, clothe yourselves with compassion, kindness, humility, gentleness and patience. (Col. 3:12)

> Love is patient, love is kind. It does not envy, it does not boast, it is not proud. It is not rude, it is not self-seeking, it is not easily angered, it keeps no record of wrongs. Love does not delight in evil but rejoices with the truth. It always protects, always trusts, always hopes, always perseveres. (1 Cor. 13:4–8)

Clothe yourself with compassion, kindness, humility, gentleness, and patience. What a wonderful description of the kind of life God wants His children to live. In 1 Corinthians 13 Paul further defined how we arrive at that kind of life when he discussed living a life of love: Love is kind. When we run our words and actions through the filter of love before we act or speak, we can then determine whether we are actually acting with the other person's best interest in mind. Commit to love. Clothe yourself with compassion and kindness. Remember the command is to be "kind to everyone." (2 Tim. 2:24). That doesn't mean everyone except the person you don't want to show kindness to. Kindness to everyone is the standard.

"The fruit of the Spirit is . . . kindness" (Gal. 5:22). It may be that if you are struggling with showing kindness, there are some issues in your life that you need to address so that God can better equip you to deal appropriately with others. Confess your struggle to God and ask Him to show you what changes you need to make. Then brace yourself for what He reveals. If we are being unkind to others, one thing we can be sure of is that the Lord's Spirit is not the one producing those attitudes and behaviors in us. Beware!

Food for thought:

- Are you being kind to everyone?
- If you know people you have been unkind to, ask God to show you what you need to do to correct the mistakes you have made and to help you to improve the way you extend kindness in the future.
- Don't fall into the trap of judging others who may not be in the same place spiritually as you are right now. Be kind to them, even if they are unkind in return.
- Father in Heaven, my prayer for my readers is that You will enable them to be open to the leading of your Spirit and that You will grant them the grace and the mercy to be able to forgive and to be kind to each person in their lives so that the message of Christ can be carried forward in their lives. In the glorious name of Jesus. Amen.

DAY TWENTY

The Fruit of the Spirit Is Goodness

Jesus was approached one day by a man who addressed him as Good Teacher. Jesus' response was that only God is good (Mark 10:17–18). As we enter into this discussion of goodness, it is important to keep in mind that God is the standard. We will always be disappointed or we will settle for less than the genuine article if we allow the focus to be on comparing ourselves with other people. Whether we may be better or worse than someone else is irrelevant. Are we growing to be more like God? Are we emulating His qualities—His goodness, His purity, His passion, etc.?

> For you were once darkness, but now you are light in the Lord. Live as children of light (for the fruit of the light consists in all goodness, righteousness and truth) and find out what pleases the Lord. Have nothing to do with the fruitless deeds of darkness, but rather expose them. For it is shameful even to mention what the disobedient do in secret. But everything exposed by the light becomes visible, for it is light that makes everything visible. This is why it is said:
>
> > "Wake up, O sleeper, rise from the dead, and Christ will shine on you."
>
> Be very careful, then, how you live—not as unwise but as wise, making the most of every opportunity, because the days are evil. Therefore do not be foolish, but understand what the Lord's will is. (Eph. 5:8–17)

The goal is to understand God's will. It's not an attempt to be holier than anyone else. We need to be focusing on our Lord and on the changes

He desires to make and the standards He sets. Please do not settle for anything less.

As we begin looking at the subject of goodness, it is crucial that we frame the discussion within the life that God calls us to live in Christ. We cannot expect the people of the world to share the same moral standards that we have. They don't serve the same Lord. We have been called out of the darkness and are called to live in the light. Yes, we can shine the light of truth and try to encourage changes to be made, but until the people we are confronting come to the place of at least acknowledging God, we are engaging in an exercise of futility to expect them to change simply because "God said so." Today's study is focusing on *us*. What should *our* standard be? While we certainly hope that the people of the world will make some better choices, we cannot compromise our standards simply because others don't (and most won't).

Josh McDowell, in his book *Right from Wrong*, presents an important concept for us. Repeatedly McDowell discusses the fact that behind every precept (command) is a principle. And behind every principle is the person of God. As you look at commands given in Scripture, look for the principle behind that command. Then once you have identified the principle, look for what that principle reveals of the character of God. As you gain a clearer picture of God's nature, your task of making good decisions will become easier because you will be able to determine more clearly how God wants your life to look based on who He is.

Let's look at one example of how this works. Consider the command "Speak the truth in love" (Eph. 4:15). There are actually two commands here. First, speak the truth. Second, do it in love. The principles revealed here are that we are to be honest and loving people. Why? Because God is truth (Hebrews 6:18 says that it is impossible for Him to lie) and because God is love (1 John 4:8). We could look at a lot more verses to demonstrate these truths, but I am sure you get the idea. Spend some time looking at these concepts. Remember, the goal is to see God more clearly.

His divine power has given us everything we need for life and godliness through our knowledge of him who called us by his own glory and goodness. Through these he has given us his very great and precious promises, so that through them you may participate in the divine nature and escape the corruption in the world caused by evil desires.

For this very reason, make every effort to add to your faith goodness; and to goodness, knowledge; and to knowledge, self-control; and to self-control, perseverance; and to perseverance, godliness; and to godliness, brotherly kindness; and to brotherly kindness, love. For if you possess these qualities in increasing measure, they will keep you from being ineffective and unproductive in your knowledge of our Lord Jesus Christ. But if anyone does not have them, he is nearsighted and blind, and has forgotten that he has been cleansed from his past sins.

Therefore, my brothers, be all the more eager to make your calling and election sure. For if you do these things, you will never fall, and you will receive a rich welcome into the eternal kingdom of our Lord and Savior Jesus Christ. (2 Peter 1:3–11)

Add to your faith goodness. The New American Standard translation says "moral excellence." What a wonderful standard for us to shoot for. Striving to demonstrate excellence in our moral stances. Again, not because we think we are better than anyone else or because we're attempting to have a holier-than-thou attitude, but because the one we serve is holy and He calls us to live holy lives. Really look at the promise made above. If you are growing in each of those areas, you will be productive and your entrance into the eternal kingdom will be richly supplied. Wow!

1 John 3:2–3 tells us that purity is not optional if we really have the hope of eternal life. Listen to John's words:

Dear friends, now we are children of God, and what we will be has not yet been made known. But we know that when he appears, we shall be like him, for we shall see him as he is. Everyone who has this hope in him purifies himself, just as he is pure.

Everyone who has the hope of the resurrection will purify himself. Moral excellence or purity is crucial if we hope to be with the Lord in heaven. Please note, however, that this is in no way talking about an attempt to try to earn our way in. This is talking about radical transformation because of a vibrant relationship with God.

The fruit that the Spirit produces is goodness (Gal. 5:22). He is the one who helps us to put to death the deeds of the flesh (Rom. 8:13). The question is this: are you sowing to the flesh or to the Spirit? (Gal. 6:7–8).

Again, remember that God is the standard. Stay focused on His character and His heart, and commit to daily following in the footsteps of Jesus.

Food for thought:

- Have you been willing to allow the standards of the world to be your standards?
- What changes do you need to make in your life to raise the standard to moral excellence?
- Are there people you have hurt because your moral standards have been too low? Is so, what can you do to remedy the situation?
- Remember the process that Josh McDowell presents in *Right from Wrong*: Behind every precept is a principle, and behind every principle is the person of God.

Day Twenty-one

The Fruit of the Spirit Is Faithfulness

Before we start looking at what it means to be faithful, I think it is important to take a look at God and His faithfulness. Prayerfully consider the following passages.

> No temptation has seized you except what is common to man. And God is faithful; he will not let you be tempted beyond what you can bear. But when you are tempted, he will also provide a way out so that you can stand up under it. (1 Cor. 10:13)

> But the Lord is faithful, and he will strengthen and protect you from the evil one. (2 Thess. 3:3)

> But as surely as God is faithful, our message to you is not "Yes" and "No." For the Son of God, Jesus Christ, who was preached among you by me and Silas and Timothy, was not "Yes" and "No," but in him it has always been "Yes." For no matter how many promises God has made, they are "Yes" in Christ. And so through him the "Amen" is spoken by us to the glory of God. Now it is God who makes both us and you stand firm in Christ. He anointed us, set his seal of ownership on us, and put his Spirit in our hearts as a deposit, guaranteeing what is to come." (2 Cor. 1:18–22)

Each of these passages talks about the faithfulness of God. He will provide a way out; He will protect you; He will keep His promises. What a huge difference between what we see revealed about God here and how most people live. The truth is that people will let us down. That's why our hope is not based on what people do. God is the standard. He is faithful! So what does that say to us as we examine the fruit of the Spirit being faithfulness (Gal. 5:22)? The first thing we need to recognize is that the Spirit is in the process of molding us to be more like God. Just because people of the world may settle for not being faithful doesn't excuse Christians from living by a higher standard. The world thinks it's OK to be unfaithful to your spouse. God disagrees. The world may not think there is a problem with being unfaithful in keeping your word. Again, God disagrees.

There have been times when people in churches have allowed faithfulness to be defined by how regularly a person attends services. Though being with believers is certainly extremely important to God and to the health of the believer, it is not the only thing people need to consider when they are evaluating faithfulness. (I'm talking about you evaluating yourself, not others).

I think we see an important piece of the puzzle when we look at the passage above in 2 Corinthians. God demonstrates His faithfulness by always keeping His word. When God makes a promise, He keeps that promise. How would your life change if every time you told someone that you were going to do something you followed through and kept your word? Learning to let your yes be yes and your no be no is how Jesus stated it. (Matt. 5:37).

Revelation 2:10b says "Be faithful, even to the point of death, and I will give you the crown of life." John said that faithfulness needed to extend even to the point of dying. Faithfulness is not something we do when circumstances make it easy. It's also not something we do simply when we feel like it. Do you really think that Jesus "felt like" going to the cross? If you do, take another look at the Garden of Gethsemane.

The encouraging thing to me is that God hasn't simply commanded us to be faithful and then left us on our own to try to figure out how to pull it off. The fruit that His Spirit produces within us is faithfulness. Yes, God commands us to be faithful. But He also equips us to be able to be faithful as well.

Food for thought:

- How have you seen God's faithfulness in providing ways out of temptation for you?
- How has His faithfulness been revealed in the promises you've seen Him keep in your life?
- Spend some time thinking about how awesome the promise is that "all of God's promises are yes in Christ." It's an amazing truth.
- Commit to being faithful both in word and in action.

Day Twenty-two

The Fruit of the Spirit Is Gentleness

God desires to produce a spirit of gentleness in each one of us. Though gentleness may come more easily to some of us than it does to others, it is a quality that God wants us to have. Today we're going to look at several passages and several ways that the idea of being gentle will affect our daily lives. Let's start with Proverbs 15:1: "A gentle answer turns away wrath, but a harsh word stirs up anger."

How many times in your life have you seen the second part of this verse played out? Someone (maybe you) became angry and gave in to the urge to blurt out seemingly the first thing that popped into his head, and the fight was on. Oh, that we could all learn the art of consistently giving a gentle answer. This doesn't mean that we won't have disagreements with other people. But how much needless pain could we avoid by simply toning down the intensity of our answers? A gentle answer. Let that be your goal.

> As a prisoner for the Lord, then, I urge you to live a life worthy of the calling you have received. Be completely humble and gentle; be patient, bearing with one another in love. Make every effort to keep the unity of the Spirit through the bond of peace." (Eph. 4:1–3)

Be completely humble and gentle. Not just a little humble or a little gentle. Completely! As we look at this command again, it is encouraging to note that gentleness is a fruit of the Spirit. We are to strive for it, but at the same time He is actively working to produce it within us. It is when we start working on it from both sides—we do our part and He does His—that we experience the best results. (Incidentally, that's true in every one of the areas concerning the fruit of the Spirit). The command is to be gentle. This does not mean be a wimp. In fact, if you look at the life of Christ, you see times when he was anything but wimpy. Remember when he cleared the temple? Genuine humility and gentleness are not equated with being weak, but being meek, having strength that is under control (more on this tomorrow).

A gentle answer. This talks about exercising some control even when tempers around us may be stirred up. We need to remain calm. This is where it is important to allow God to help transform temperaments. Even if you have been given to losing your temper, God can help you get that under control. But you have to be willing to surrender and start living life based on His terms, allowing Him to change you from the inside out. Seek His counsel and His transforming power.

Let's look at Philippians 4:5–7 next:

> Let your gentleness be evident to all. The Lord is near. Do not be anxious about anything, but in everything, by prayer and petition, with thanksgiving, present your requests to God. And the peace of God, which transcends all understanding, will guard your hearts and your minds in Christ Jesus.

Let the world see your gentleness. Don't hide it. Isn't it great that Paul followed the command with the assurance that the Lord is near us? You don't have to try to do this alone. If you are anxious about your temper, pray about it. If you are anxious about your relationships, again, pray. Whatever the requests, give them with thanksgiving and the promise is that God will provide a wonderful measure of peace.

Next let's look at Colossians 3:12: "Therefore, as God's chosen people, holy and dearly loved, clothe yourselves with compassion, kindness, humility, gentleness and patience."

Clothe yourself with compassion, kindness, humility, gentleness and patience. Those aren't qualities that people outside of Christ often think of as being important. But God wants us to live a radically different lifestyle. Not for the sake of simply being different, but for the sake of being a blessing to others and to enable us to help draw others to Him. Clothe yourself with gentleness.

1 Timothy 6:11 tells us to pursue righteousness, godliness, faith, love, endurance, and gentleness. How actively have you been pursuing any of these, but specifically today, how actively are you pursuing gentleness? It is important for us to see where we are in our spiritual growth if we want to really understand what the whole concept of returning to innocence concerning evil means in our daily lives. We can't return to innocence if we don't first recognize the areas in our lives where we need work.

I'd like to look at one more passage today. "But in your hearts set apart Christ as Lord. Always be prepared to give an answer to everyone who asks you to give the reason for the hope that you have. But do this with gentleness and respect" (1 Peter 3:15–16). I'm begging you to listen to what Peter says here. Whenever anyone asks you to give a reason for why you have hope, always be ready with an answer, but let the answer be given *with gentleness and respect.* Unfortunately, numerous times I've seen people tell others exactly why they had hope, but either their answers were given in a harsh or judgmental spirit or they showed absolutely no respect for the person they were talking to, and a tremendous amount of damage was needlessly done to the relationship. Yes, we are to stand up for the truth. Yes, we are to combat false teaching when confronted with it, but we don't have to be ugly or cruel when confronted with these situations. Sometimes we may have to learn to be more like Jesus was when confronted with people who were not interested in listening to Him. They just wanted to accuse; His response was to remain silent. Let's pray for the wisdom to know when to answer and the strength to be able to answer gently so that those who hear us can focus more on the message than the messenger.

Food for thought:

- Are you actively pursuing gentleness in your life?
- Spend some time evaluating the passages we've discussed today and see what changes God wants to make in your life.
- Spend some time praying and asking God to help you make the changes you've identified.

Day Twenty-three

The Fruit of the Spirit Is Self-Control

Self-control is not something we spend much time thinking about, is it? It's a concept we probably don't want to spend much time on because it doesn't allow for the excuses we want so desperately to believe. Paul said that even though things were "lawful" they were not necessarily beneficial. He went on to say, "I will not be mastered by anything" (1 Cor. 6:12). So before we really delve into our topic today, let me ask this question: Are there things in your life (other than God) that have mastered you? Whether it is eating habits, or sexual immorality, or anger, if it has become your master, it is sinful. Today we look at the idea that God has commanded us to live self-controlled lives, but He also equips us to live that way.

> Several days later Felix came with his wife Drusilla, who was a Jewess. He sent for Paul and listened to him as he spoke about faith in Christ Jesus. . . . Paul discoursed on righteousness, self-control and the judgment to come. (Acts 24:24–25a)

When Paul was presenting his case to Felix, three things he felt were important to cover: righteousness, self-control, and judgment. Most of this book has been dealing with righteousness in one way or another, but there is an important element that we miss if we fail to grasp the critical role that self-control plays in our lives. If you sit down to do a family budget and you want to accurately discern the state of your finances, there are a couple of things that you have to find out. How much is coming in? And how much is going out? Many times when people start figuring out a budget they focus only on what they can do to bring in more money. Though this is an important part of the equation, they may be overlooking the crucial part. Any successful budget will ultimately come down to this: spend less than you make. Learn to exercise some self-control and get the spending under control so that whatever budget you come up with will work.

> But you, brothers, are not in darkness so that this day should surprise you like a thief. You are all sons of the light and sons of the day. We do not belong to the night or to the darkness. So then, let us not be like others, who are asleep, but let us be alert and self-controlled. For those who sleep, sleep at night, and those who get drunk, get drunk at night. But since we belong to the day, let us be self-controlled, putting on faith and love as a breastplate, and the hope of salvation as a helmet. For God did not appoint us to suffer wrath but to receive salvation through our Lord Jesus Christ. He died for us so that, whether we are awake or asleep, we may live together with him. Therefore encourage one another and build each other up, just as in fact you are doing. (1 Thess. 5:4–11).

We belong to the light! What a wonderful statement. Since that's true, let us learn to be self-controlled. People living in darkness are out of control. They live their lives for the joy of the moment, constantly seeking the next thrill. Living out of control is not God's will for your life. This passage reminds us that this life is only temporary and that we are heading for our eternal destiny. Christ died for you to rescue you from a life that was out of control and without hope. His purpose was to bring you into the light and to equip you to regain a measure of control and sanity in your life. He doesn't want you to merely exist in this life, but to live life and live it to the full (John 10:10).

Let's look at part of what God says He desires from our lives:

> It is God's will that you should be sanctified: that you should avoid sexual immorality; that each of you should learn to control his own body in a way that is holy and honorable, not in passionate lust like the heathen, who do not know God; and that in this matter no one should wrong his brother or take advantage of him. The Lord will punish men for all such sins, as we have already told you and warned

you. For God did not call us to be impure, but to live a holy life. Therefore, he who rejects this instruction does not reject man but God, who gives you his Holy Spirit. (1 Thess. 4:3–8)

It is God's will that you should be set apart (sanctified) for His work, that you should learn to control your body in a way that is holy and honorable. In fact, He called you to live a holy life. Here comes the real kicker: If we reject the instruction to live a holy life, we are not rejecting men, we're rejecting God who gives us His Holy Spirit. Self-control and striving for a holy life are not simply items in the cafeteria of life that we can either accept or reject. If we want to be pleasing to God they are essential.

When Paul wrote to Titus he gave him the following admonitions:

> For the grace of God that brings salvation has appeared to all men. It teaches us to say "No" to ungodliness and worldly passions, and to live self-controlled, upright and godly lives in this present age, while we wait for the blessed hope—the glorious appearing of our great God and Savior, Jesus Christ, who gave himself for us to redeem us from all wickedness and to purify for himself a people that are his very own, eager to do what is good. (Titus 2:11–14)

Paul told Titus that God's grace teaches us not to be like the world and to start exercising self-controlled, upright and godly lives. That needs to be our aim today as well. Don't settle for mediocrity. Don't fall into the trap of comparing yourself with the people around you. Even if you do have more self-control than the unsaved people around you, so what? Don't compare yourself with the world. Look at what God wants to produce within you, and live your life in order to exalt His glorious name.

In 1 Peter 1:13, Peter wrote these words: "Therefore, prepare your minds for action; be self-controlled; set your hope fully on the grace to be given you when Jesus Christ is revealed." Prepare your mind for action. Cultivate some self-control. And set your hope on the grace you receive in Christ. What wonderful advice.

Is your life an example of self-control?

Food for thought:

- As we have examined the various Scriptures today, have you identified some areas where you life is out of control?
- What changes do you need to ask God to help you make in order to surrender fully to His plans for you?
- Are there areas that are out of control that maybe you don't really want to change? If so, they are a problem and they need to be addressed. Remember, Paul talked about things that may well be "lawful" (they may be perfectly all right by themselves) but if they have mastered us they have become sinful. I'm begging you to repent. Ask the Lord to help you to regain freedom so that you can be a shining example of life in the light.

GETTING PRACTICAL

DAY TWENTY-FOUR

Overcoming Compulsive Behavior

It would be great if all destructive habits simply vanished when a person came to Christ, but that was not true in the early days of the church, nor is it true now. The truth is that many Christians struggle with inner compulsions of one kind or another. Some of these compulsions include stress, work, emotions, pornography, sex, overeating, anger, alcohol, drugs, selfishness, self-pity, and perfection.[31] A Christian is not automatically wise about good or instantly innocent about evil simply because he has been cleansed from his past sins.

Simply put, compulsive behavior can mean being overcome by some inner struggle. The result is a feeling of helplessness when confronted with something that seems to be irresistible.[32] Compulsive behavior is devastating to many people's lives and is a very common experience.[33]

If compulsive desires are so common and include such a wide range of areas of temptation, how can Christians deal with them effectively? The answer begins by our letting go of the false notion that we can handle things by themselves. Lester Sumrall states that as long as a person hangs onto this false notion, he is dooming himself to failure.[34]

To illustrate, we are going to take a closer look at alcoholism. However, the principles can be applied to any area of addiction or compulsive behavior. Erwin Letzer states that alcoholics can't handle even one drink.[35] Unfortunately the cycle that the alcoholic goes through is a very common one. Whether it is using pornography, gambling, overeating, or drinking, pride tends to follow the first successes in resisting temptation. Once a person has had a victory, he begins to think the war has been won, but he is actually only a step away from the enemy's most deadly ambush.[36]

Solomon, in writing Proverbs 11:2, told us that pride comes before a fall. Paul warned the church in Rome that they should not think too highly of themselves, but rather they ought to think with sober judgment (Rom. 12:3). So Many Christians fail because they feel like they can handle their problems alone. We can't!

Alcoholics Anonymous uses a twelve-step program for helping its members to overcome alcohol, which has been adapted to help with many different types of addiction.[37] Here are the twelve steps:

1. Admit that you are powerless over alcohol.
2. Believe that a Power greater than you can restore you to sanity.
3. Make a decision to turn your will and life over to God (as you view Him).
4. Make a searching and fearless moral inventory of yourself.
5. Admit to God and to yourself the exact nature of your wrongs.
6. You must be completely ready to have God remove all of your defects of character.
7. Humbly ask God to remove your shortcomings.
8. Make a list of all the people that you have harmed and be willing to make amends to all of them.
9. Make direct amends to these people when it is possible to do so. (Do not do so if it would harm them or others).

10. Continue to take a personal inventory and when you have done wrong, promptly admit it.
11. Through prayer and meditation, seek to improve your conscious contact with God. Pray for knowledge of His will for you and the power to carry it out.
12. Now that you have carried out these 12 steps, try to carry the message of this spiritual awakening to others who are struggling and then practice these same principles in every aspect of your life.[38]

The alcoholic, in facing his struggles, needs to begin in the same place that anyone does to truly overcome sin. It begins with poverty of spirit. Without the recognition that a person needs God's help, he is powerless to overcome his struggle. That is why Jesus reveals that the process begins with being poor in spirit and then continues with mourning because of sin. Meekness and hungering and thirsting for righteousness follow the mourning. Being merciful follows these and they all precede purity of heart" (Matt. 5:8).

In the same way that Jesus taught that there is a definite order to spiritual maturity, Alcoholics Anonymous and other groups have shown that there are definite steps necessary to overcoming compulsive behavior. Lester Sumrall says that a very important aspect of overcoming sin is the willingness to accept responsibility for your sin.[39] He goes on to say that it is absolutely essential in overcoming compulsive desires to admit that we struggle.[40] He also says that the way that we respond to temptation shows, better than anything else does, what our commitment level truly is.[41] It is when a Christian begins to successfully deal with temptation that he grows to be more like Christ.[42]

A.W. Tozer says, "No Christian ever fell into sin who did not first allow himself to brood over it with increasing desire."[43] This is certainly in keeping with what James taught when he wrote that each person is tempted by his own evil desire. Then after the desire is conceived, sin is born (James 1:13–15). He is saying that when a person begins to think about a sin, the seed has been planted. After he thinks it over for a while, the desire begins to grow, and then the desire changes to action. This process shows us why it is vital for us to renew our thinking as we discussed in the chapter on renewing our mind.

Though there are those who need to enroll themselves in an organized twelve-step program to overcome the sins they struggle with, it is certainly not necessary for everyone. We will deal with some other ways of dealing with sin in our study tomorrow.

Food for thought:

- Please don't gloss over this section. If you struggle with recurring sin, whether it is alcohol, pornography, drugs, lying, or any other sin, give careful thought to the concepts presented today.
- Find as many passages as you can that deal with the area that you are most tempted in. Memorize them. Pray for God to help you to stay as far from known places of temptation as you can.
- Seek professional help if needed.
- Find a brother or sister in Christ that you are willing to be accountable to, and ask the person to check on you regularly to be able to help you to be victorious over this sin.
- Pray, pray, pray. God can help you to overcome!
- Remember that Satan is a liar and that the lies he will tell you about not being able to overcome are just that—lies.

Day Twenty-five

The Replacement Principle

Today we will look at a process that should be involved every time a Christian realizes that there is sin in his life. The first step in this process is the same as with any problem we confront in life. Before the problem can effectively be dealt with, it must be identified. This is where we need to allow the Lord to shine the light of truth on every area of sin that needs to be exposed. The more specific we can be in identifying exactly what needs to be removed, the more effective we will be in getting rid of it. Once the root of the sin has been accurately identified, the second step needs to take place, namely, repent! We will look in more detail at what the Scriptures teach about repentance, and then finally, we will examine the very important subject of replacement.

Identify

> For we are the temple of the living God. As God has said: "I will live with them and walk among them, and I will be their God, and they will be my people. Therefore come out from them and be separate," says the Lord. "Touch no unclean thing, and I will receive you. I will be a Father to you, and you will be my sons and daughters, says the Lord Almighty."
>
> Since we have these promises, dear friends, let us purify ourselves from everything that contaminates body and spirit, perfecting holiness out of reverence for God. (2 Cor. 6:16–7:1)

To be able to purify himself from "everything that contaminates," a believer must first know what it is that contaminates his body or his spirit.

To illustrate how this process works in the physical realm, suppose a family is having financial difficulties and wants to be able to pay off their debts. To get a handle on the debt situation, they need to get an accurate picture of what they are really facing. The husband and wife might get together to look at exactly how much income they have. Then they would gather all of their bills to see how much money is needed each month to be able to pay each bill on time. Then they need to examine where the money is actually being spent each month. They may find that money is being wasted. For example, they might see that they have been eating out a lot. To cut back on their spending they might decide to eat out less so that their bill payments can be made. The more specific they can be in this part of the process the better they will be able to set up a workable budget that will accomplish the goal of being able to pay their bills on time.

The same thing is true in the spiritual arena. The closer the believer wants to grow to God, the more he needs to examine himself to identify everything that would damage his relationship with God. The more specific he is in identifying the things that contaminate and separate the more effective he can be in removing them.

Repent

Throughout the Bible, when a person is confronted with sin, the Lord always desires the same response. He wants them to repent. So what does that mean? *The American Heritage Dictionary* defines it this way: "to feel contrition for one's sins and to abjure sinful ways." Ethelbert Bullinger states that repentance carries with it the idea of reformation and having a genuine change of heart and life from worse to better.[44]

> Now there were some present at that time who told Jesus about the Galileans whose blood Pilate had mixed with their sacrifices. Jesus answered, "Do you think that these Galileans were worse sinners than all the other Galileans because they suffered this way?" I tell you, no! But unless you repent, you too will all perish. Or those eighteen who died when the tower in Siloam fell on them—do you think they were

more guilty than all the others living in Jerusalem? I tell you, no! But unless you repent, you too will all perish." (Luke 13:1–5)

Now, brothers, I know that you acted in ignorance, as did your leaders. But this is how God fulfilled what he had foretold through all the prophets, saying that his Christ would suffer. Repent, then, and turn to God, so that your sins may be wiped out, that times of refreshing may come from the Lord, and that he may send the Christ, who has been appointed for you—even Jesus. (Acts 3:17–20)

In Acts 8:13, Simon, a man who had practiced sorcery, believed and was baptized. However, he still struggled with some sinful motives and was told by Peter that he had "no part or share in this ministry, because your heart is not right before God" (Acts 8:21). In verse 22 Peter told him to repent of the wickedness and to pray. "Perhaps he will forgive you for having such a thought in your heart. For I see that you are full of bitterness and captive to sin." This man, according to verse thirteen, was a baptized believer in Christ and yet he was full of bitterness and had sin that had to be repented of in order to be forgiven.

In Acts 17:30 Paul preached that God now "commands all people everywhere to repent." John, in writing to the seven churches of Asia made the following statements:

Remember the height from which you have fallen! Repent and do the things you did at first. If you do not repent, I will come to you and remove your lampstand from its place. (Rev. 2:5)

Likewise you also have those who hold to the teaching of the Nicolaitans. Repent therefore! Otherwise, I will soon come to you and will fight against them with the sword of my mouth. (Rev. 2:15–16)

Nevertheless, I have this against you: You tolerate that woman Jezebel, who calls herself a prophetess. By her teaching she misleads my servants into sexual immorality and the eating of food sacrificed to idols.

I have given her time to repent of her immorality, but she is unwilling. So I will cast her on a bed of suffering, and I will make those who commit adultery with her suffer intensely, unless they repent of her ways. (Rev. 2:20–22)

Remember, therefore, what you have received and heard; obey it, and repent. But if you do not wake up, I will come like a thief, and you will not know at what time I will come to you. (Rev. 3:3)

Those whom I love I rebuke and discipline. So be earnest, and repent. (Rev. 3:19)

In these passages the recurring theme is that every time a believer or a non-believer is confronted with sin they are commanded to repent. This is still true today. If the believer wants to be wise about good, he must cultivate the ongoing commitment to repent every time he recognizes that there is sin in his life.

After the Christian identifies the sin in his life and then turns away from it (repents), another step in the cleansing process needs to be addressed. To introduce this step let's look at a principle that Jesus taught in Luke 11:24–26:

When an evil spirit comes out of a man, it goes through arid places seeking rest and does not find it. Then it says, "I will return to the house I left." When it arrives, it finds the house swept clean and put in order. Then it goes and takes seven other spirits more wicked than itself, and they go in and live there. And the final condition of that man is worse than the first.

If we examine the principle being taught in this passage, we will see something that is very important in dealing with sin, as well as what Jesus said about the evil spirits. The mind is not simply a vacuum. This could be called the "replacement principle." After a person repents of sin and turns to God, then, rather than simply leaving the space empty and hoping for the best, the believer needs to fill that time and space with things that are true, noble, right, pure, lovely, admirable, excellent, or praiseworthy (Phil. 4:8). This principle is also taught in the passages that were discussed in the chapter on renewing your mind. For meaningful growth it is vital for the Christian to replace sinful thoughts with pure thoughts. As Paul told the church in Corinth, "Take every thought captive to make it obedient to Christ" (2 Cor. 10:5).

Another part of the spiritual healing process taught in the Bible is that sin must be confessed. James wrote these words: "Therefore, confess your sins to each other and pray for each other so that you may be healed" (James 5:16). Though the context is dealing with physical healing, it would certainly include emotional and spiritual healing. The disciple of Christ has certainly made a lot of progress toward being wise about good and innocent about evil when he has learned to identify sin in his life, repent of it, confess it to a brother or sister in Christ, and replace it with pure thoughts and deeds.

Tomorrow we will examine how study and application of the Word of God helps in the process of replacing sin and returning to innocence.

Food for thought:

- This may very well be the most important principle in this book. Every time you find sin in your life, repent and replace.
- Get rid of the behavior and then cultivate new habits, new thought patterns, new desires.
- Memorize Philippians 4:8 and constantly check your thoughts and your behavior in light of what it teaches. When considering what to do, ask yourself: Is it true? Is it noble? Is it right? Is it pure? Is it lovely? Is it admirable? Is it excellent? Is it worthy of praise? If your answer to any on these is no, then stay away.

Day Twenty-six

Study

How can a young man keep his way pure? By living according to your word. (Ps. 119:9)

Jesus full of the Holy Spirit, returned from the Jordan and was led by the Spirit in the desert, where for forty days he was tempted by the devil. He ate nothing during those days, and at the end of them he was hungry.

The devil said to him, "If you are the Son of God, tell this stone to become bread."

Jesus answered, "It is written: 'Man does not live on bread alone.'"

The devil led him up to a high place and showed him in an instant all the kingdoms of the world. And he said to him, "I will give you all their authority and splendor, for it has been given to me, and I can give it to anyone I want to. So if you worship me, it will all be yours."

Jesus answered, "It is written: 'Worship the Lord your God and serve him only.'"

The devil led him to Jerusalem and had him stand on the highest point of the temple. "If you are the Son of God," he said, "throw yourself down from here. For it is written:

'He will command his angels concerning you to guard you carefully; they will lift you up in their hands, so that you will not strike your foot against a stone.'" Jesus answered, "It says: 'Do not put the Lord your God to the test.'" (Luke 4:1–12)

Jesus knew the Word of God and used it in confronting temptation. If the Son of God thought it was important to learn the Word of God, shouldn't we? In the passage above we have three instances in which Satan tempted our Lord, and in all three instances Jesus answered him with the Word of God. He did not have to say something like, "I know the Bible says something about this." No! He already knew what it said.

To truly be wise about good and innocent about evil the Christian must prepare ahead of time by feeding on the words that God has provided in the Bible. Psalm 119:9 tells us that the believer keeps pure by following the Word of God.

In a poll done by George Gallup it was revealed that eighty-nine percent of all Americans do not read their Bibles on a daily basis. The poll showed that though many people revere the Bible, most of them don't actually read it. Even many Christians do not read the Bible very often. Many of those who do read it, do not read it enough to change their lives.[45] We are not talking about studying the Bible out of a sense of duty but rather spending time feeding on the Word out of a desire to be more like Jesus. In fact, if we want to be like Him, we must spend regular time talking to God as He did as well as feasting on His word to learn His will for our lives, just as Jesus did.

In Matthew 5:6 Jesus said that the people who "hunger and thirst for righteousness" would be filled. This is the attitude of the heart that is needed to grow close to God. The absolutely amazing promise given in this verse is that with this attitude the believer "will be filled."

However, there is a danger involved in studying for the wrong reasons. Paul had to warn the church in Corinth about the fact that "knowledge puffs up" (1 Cor. 8:1). He contrasted this kind of knowledge with love which he said "builds up." If the Christian is studying to merely gain head knowledge or to try to win a spiritual or theological argument, beware. The motives are wrong.

As we discussed earlier, God is the only source of good. If anyone desires to be wise about good then it only makes sense to go to the words that God has revealed about Himself. 2 Timothy 3:16–17 says, "All Scripture is God-breathed and is useful for teaching, rebuking, correcting and training in righteousness, so that the man of God may be thoroughly equipped for every good work." If the believer wants to be completely "equipped for every good work," he needs to study the only book that has the power to equip him.

Why does the Bible have this power? Because, unlike any other book,

> the word of God is living and active. Sharper than any double-edged sword, it penetrates even to dividing soul and spirit, joints and marrow; it judges the thoughts and attitudes of the heart. Nothing in all creation is hidden from God's sight. Everything is uncovered and laid bare before the eyes of him to whom we must give account. (Heb. 4:12–13).

Since the Bible is the inspired Word of God and it has the power, as a living document, to judge the heart, it makes sense for the serious follower of Christ to devote himself to learning all that he can about it. This will allow the Lord to use it to mold the disciple to be more like his Lord and Savior Jesus Christ.

There are two powerful aids to returning to innocence: prayer and Bible study. (We will examine prayer as a part of this process on another day.) One way that Bible study helps is that it enables us to know the will of God and shows us what purity of life is all about.

We will go in to more detail tomorrow where we will be studying the subject of meditation.

Food for thought:

- I once had an English teacher who said there are two ways to read a book. You can either read it to see what it says, or you can read it to see what it is saying.
- As you study the Bible, please don't ever read just to see what it says. Look much deeper to identify what it is saying.
- Pray for the Lord to help you to understand what you're studying. Spend time thinking about what it says about the Lord and about you life.
- Make the commitment to be a doer of the word and not just a hearer only (James 1:22).

Day Twenty-seven

Meditate

Meditation, often misunderstood because of the various oriental and New Age influences, is a spiritual discipline that is often overlooked in the church. To begin the discussion we need to see what God has revealed on this topic in His word.

> I rejoice in following your statutes as one rejoices in great riches. I mediate on your precepts and consider your ways. (Ps. 119:14–15)

> Though rulers sit together and slander me, your servant will meditate on your decrees. Your statutes are my delight; they are my counselors. (Ps. 119:23–24)

> Let me understand the teaching of your precepts; then I will mediate on your wonders." (Ps. 119:27)

> I lift up my hands to your commands, which I love, and I mediate on your decrees." (Ps. 119:48)

> May the arrogant be put to shame for wronging me without cause; but I will meditate on your precepts." (Ps. 119:78)

> My eyes stay open through the watches of the night, that I may meditate on your promises." (Ps. 119:148)

In the first of these passages that use the word "meditate" it involves a quiet reflection on God's works as well as on God's Word. In the second instance it is described as "rehearsing aloud God's words."[46]

Another form of the word "meditate" is in Psalm 119:97, 99:

Oh, how I love your law! I meditate on it all day long. Your commands make me wiser than my enemies, for they are ever with me. I have more insight than all my teachers, for I meditate on your statutes.

The word that is translated "meditation" here is used only three times in the Old Testament and carries with it the idea of "pious meditation."[47]

What was the psalmist meditating about? In verses fifteen and seventy-eight it was the precepts of God; in verses twenty-three and forty-eight it was God's decrees. Verse twenty-seven says he meditated on the wonders of God, and in verse 148 he meditated on God's promises. His meditation was on the law of God in verse ninety-seven, and he meditated on the statutes of God in verse ninety-nine.

What these verses are all saying is that his mind was focused on God and that he was constantly thinking about or dwelling on what God wanted for his life. What a valuable lesson for us!

The Christian who wants to cultivate a closer relationship with God would be wise to develop a regular time and place for getting away from distractions to meditate on the things that God has written in His word.[48] When meditating on the Word of God, the Christian is contemplating what God desires of his life. This is a time for prayerful thought and consideration, for examination, for looking for direction, and for listening for instruction. Though meditation is primarily us looking to God for answers, please don't allow this to merely become another ritual that you go through to look or to act "spiritual." Our goal is to become genuinely wise about good and innocent about evil.

Today we've looked at the subject of meditation to learn more of God's will for our lives. Tomorrow we will discuss the topic of prayer and how it helps us in our growth.

Food for thought:

- Please don't let the word "meditate" scare you. We're not talking about some kind of chanting or mystical ceremonies. We are talking about a deep sense of contemplation concerning the things of God. Spend time really wrestling with what God has revealed to us in His Word and what it means for your life.
- Take the time to meditate on God's commands.
- Meditate on His character.
- Meditate on what His Word reveals concerning your life.

Day Twenty-eight

Pray

This study is designed to help Christians learn how they can return to innocence concerning evil and how they can learn to be wise about what is good. Instead of relying on his own strength, the believer needs to realize that he can take his weaknesses and needs to God and ask for His help. In the following passages we will see a few of the areas we are told to pray about. Also we will see examples of spiritual needs that others have brought before the Father's throne.

If any of you lacks wisdom, he should ask God, who gives generously to all without finding fault, and it will be given to him. (James 1:5)

So I say to you: Ask and it will be given to you; seek and you will find; knock and the door will be opened to you. For everyone who asks receives; he who seeks finds; and to him who knocks, the door will be opened.

Which of you Fathers, if your son asks for a fish, will give him a snake instead? Or it he asks for an egg, will give him s scorpion? If you then, though you are evil, know how to give good gifts to your children, how much more will your Father in heaven give the Holy Spirit to those who ask him! (Luke 11:9–3)

Praise be to you, O LORD; teach me your decrees. (Ps. 119:12)

Teach me, O LORD, to follow your decrees; then I will keep them to the end." (Ps. 119:33)

Give me understanding, and I will keep your law and obey it with all my heart. (Ps. 119:34)

Turn my heart toward your statutes and not toward selfish gain. (Ps. 119:36)

These passages show us how much the psalmist was willing to acknowledge his absolute need for God. With statements like: "give me understanding" and "teach me your decrees," it is easy to see how much the writer felt his own inadequacy and his need for God to be actively involved in his spiritual development. The believer today should cultivate that same heart for the Lord. Instead of trying to be self-sufficient and becoming a "self made" Christian—surrender to God! Approach the Lord the way the disciples did and say, "Lord, teach me to pray" (Luke 11:1).

Many of the tasks that have already been discussed in this study would be impossible to do without God's help. If the believer wants to truly renew his mind, he would be foolish to attempt to develop a spiritual mindset without spending time praying about what God wants him to become. When we consider the work of the Holy Spirit, we see that He is actively involved even in the prayers of the believer. "We do not know what we ought to pray for, but the Spirit Himself intercedes for us with groans that words cannot express" (Rom. 8:26). If the Christian wants to completely overcome compulsive behavior in his life he must learn to consistently take these struggles before the Father's throne. The replacement principle would also be difficult, if not impossible, without being willing to pray for wisdom and guidance from God. Study and meditation are greatly enhanced when the disciple is willing to actively seek guidance from God by asking for His involvement and direction. The spiritual growth of the disciple of Christ will be much easier and much more meaningful if he will learn to do like the apostles did in Acts 6:4. They devoted themselves to prayer and to the ministry of the word.

Listen to Paul's admonition to the church in Ephesus when he told them about spiritual armor.

Finally, be strong in the Lord and in his mighty power. Put on the full armor of God so that you can take your stand against the devil's schemes. For our struggle is not against flesh and blood, but against the rulers, against the authorities, against the powers of this dark world and against the spiritual forces of evil in the heavenly realms. Therefore put on the full armor of God, so that when the day of evil comes, you may be able to stand your ground, and after you have done everything, to stand. Stand firm then, with the belt of truth buckled around your waist, with the breastplate of righteousness in place, and with your feet fitted with the readiness that comes from the gospel of peace. In addition to all this, take up the shield of faith, with which you can extinguish all the flaming arrows of the evil one. Take the helmet of salvation and the sword of the Spirit, which is the word of God. And pray in the Spirit on all occasions with all prayers and requests. With this in mind, be alert and always keep on praying for all the saints.

Pray also for me, that whenever I open my mouth, words my be given me so that I will fearlessly make known the mystery of the gospel, for which I am an ambassador in chains. Pray that I may declare it fearlessly, as I should. (Eph. 6:10–20)

After telling the church about the wonderful armor that God has provided for Christians to be able to withstand the attacks of the enemy, Paul admonishes them to pray, pray, pray. This is still marvelous advice. To learn to be wise about good—pray! To learn to be truly innocent about evil—pray! In writing to the church at Thessalonica, Paul wrote these words: "Rejoice always, pray without ceasing; in everything give thanks; for this is God's will for you in Christ Jesus" (1 Thess. 5:16–18, NASB). Christians would be wise to follow this advice. Pray, pray, pray—and in every situation give thanks!

Tomorrow we will look at the importance of self-examination and using it to help us to return to innocence.

Food for thought:

- Please don't ever settle for simply thinking about prayer, or studying about prayer. Commit yourself to becoming a person of prayer.
- The disciples came to Jesus and said "Lord, teach us to pray" (Luke 11:1). Do the same. Ask the Lord to teach you to be a person who is devoted to praying.
- There is no substitute for praying. When in doubt—pray. When happy—pray. When sad—pray. When in need of direction—pray. But realize that praying just for the sake of praying is not what we are talking about. We're talking about cultivating a vibrant relationship with God. Don't settle for anything less.

Day Twenty-nine

Examine Yourself

For we are the temple of the living God. As God has said: "I will live with them and walk among them, and I will be their God, and they will be my people.

"Therefore come out from them and be separate, says the Lord. Touch no unclean thing, and I will receive you."

"I will be a Father to you, and you will be my sons and daughters," says the Lord Almighty.

Since we have these promises, dear friends, let us purify ourselves from everything that contaminates body and spirit, perfecting holiness out of reverence for God." (2 Cor. 6:16–7:1)

But you are a chosen people, a royal priesthood, a holy nation, a people belonging to God, that you may declare the praises of him who called you out of darkness into his wonderful light. Once you were not a people, but now you are the people of God' once you had not received mercy, but now you have received mercy.

Dear friends, I urge you, as aliens and strangers in the world, to abstain from sinful desires, which war against your soul. (1 Peter 2:9–11)

But the day of the Lord will come like a thief. The heavens will disappear with a roar; the elements will be destroyed by fire, and the earth and everything in it will be laid bare.

Since everything will be destroyed in this way, what kind of people ought you to be? You ought to live holy and godly lives as you look forward to the day of God and speed its coming. (2 Peter 3:10–12a)

Some extremely important goals are presented in the passages above. In 2 Corinthians, Paul admonished the church to "be separate." Peter wrote that we are called to "be holy," and that Christians should live "holy and godly lives."

When Jesus was preaching the Sermon on the Mount he said that those who are "pure in heart" would see God (Matt. 5:8). So a good question for the truly committed Christian to ask would be, Am I living a holy, godly, and pure life? In the book of Lamentations we can read the following admonition. "Let us examine our ways and test them, and let us return to the LORD" (Lam. 3:40).

As a person begins to examine himself there are other questions that can be extremely beneficial. We will look at a few of these.

In 2 Corinthians 7:1 Paul admonished believers to purify themselves from everything that contaminates either body or spirit. A question the Christian can ask himself when considering any given issue could be, Does this contaminate my body or my spirit? If the answer is yes, then get rid or it, or avoid it.[49]

Philippians 4:8 says, "Finally, brothers, whatever is true, whatever is noble, whatever is right, whatever is pure, whatever is lovely, whatever is admirable—if anything is excellent or praiseworthy—think about such things." The obvious questions would be, Is it true? Is it noble? Is it right? Is it pure? Is it lovely? Is it admirable? Is it excellent? Is it praiseworthy? If the answer to any of these is no, then the Christian should stay away from it.

The heart that God is looking for is like the one David displayed when he wrote the following words. "Search me, O God, and know my heart; test me and know my anxious thoughts. See if there is any offensive way in me, and lead me in the way everlasting" (Ps. 139:23–24).

If a person really wants to be wise about good and innocent about evil, then the response to what God commands should always be the same: obedience! In fact Jesus said, "If you love me, you will obey what I command." Though a person may say the words "I love Jesus," Jesus basically says, "Actions speak louder than words."

How can a person prepare himself to always be ready to obey God's will? We will examine this question further tomorrow as we examine the topic of memorizing the word of God.

Food for thought:

- To make meaningful change in our lives, we have to be brutally honest with ourselves. Ask the Lord to help you as you examine yourself. Ask Him to show you anything in your heart or your life that is still preventing you from a close walk with Him.
- Please don't pull back if the truth is ugly. If you come to realize that there are some really vile things that are a part of your life, don't get discouraged. God still loves you. He still wants fellowship with you. He can still forgive you.
- Identify the sin. Repent of it. Confess it. Replace it. Commit to walking in the light rather than going back to the darkness (1 John 1:7).
- Realize that the one who is in you is greater than the one who is in the world (1 John 4:4). Since you are in Christ, you don't have to go through life constantly being defeated by your enemy. You can do all things through Christ who gives you strength (Phil. 4:13).

Day Thirty

Memorize

> How can a young man keep his way pure? By living according to your word. I seek you with all my heart; do not let me stray from your commands. I have hidden your word in my heart that I might not sin against you. Praise be to you, O LORD; teach me your decrees. With my lips I recount all the laws that come from your mouth. I rejoice in following your statutes as one rejoices in great riches. I meditate on your precepts and consider your ways. I delight in your decrees; I will not neglect your word." (Ps. 119:9–16)

This passage shows us not only the reason to memorize God's Word but it also teaches some important insights into how it can be done. The reason to memorize God's Word is so that the believer will "not sin against Him" (vs. 11). If a person wants to know what pleases God, they will find the answer in His Word. How can a Christian hide the Word of God in his heart? Memorize it! That is how Jesus was able to withstand the temptations that Satan threw at Him in the wilderness. Each time the temptation came, the answer was, "It is written." If Jesus had to study and learn the Word of God, how much more important should it be for His followers?

Look at some of the statements that the psalmist made about hiding God's Word in his heart. In verse ten he said, "I will seek you with all my heart." Whenever a person seeks anything with all his heart it is obviously very important to him. If God's Word is that important to the believer it will be much easier to learn what it says. In verse eleven the motivation was revealed—to keep from sinning against God. In verse thirteen a wonderful method for memorization is given: "I recount all the laws that come from your mouth." Repetition is a wonderful learning tool. Vocalize, over and over, the passages that are important and keep doing so until they are hidden in the heart. Verse fifteen talks about meditation and consideration of the Word of God. The Christian should spend time dwelling on what God has said. This passage reveals both parts of what we have been studying. How a Christian can learn to be wise about good is revealed in verse nine: "How can a young man keep his way pure? By living according to your word." How the Christian can be innocent about evil is addressed in verse eleven: "I have hidden your word in my heart that I might not sin against you."

Tomorrow we will examine several spiritual exercises that can also help in this growth process.

Food for thought:

- ■ "I have hidden your word in my heart that I might not sin against you" (Ps. 119:11).
- ■ Our goal in memorizing Scripture is not so we can say that we memorized a certain number of verses. The goal is "that I might not sin against you."
- ■ As you identify any area of your life where you struggle with sin, find Scriptures dealing with that subject and hide them in your heart so that you won't go on sinning against God.

Day Thirty-one

Spiritual Exercises

Fasting

Throughout the Bible the subject of fasting is mentioned. Though people fasted for various reasons, ranging from mourning a death (1 Sam. 31:13) to fasting as a part of worship and seeking direction from God (Acts 13:2). In this part of the study we are going to focus on fasting as a discipline that can assist us in drawing closer to God.

In Nehemiah 9:1–2 the Israelites gathered together and fasted wearing sackcloth and ashes. They had sinned against God and fasted as a sign of contrition. They fasted and confessed the sins they had committed. This is a powerful expression of the attitude of heart that Jesus dealt with in Matthew 5:4 when He said: "Blessed are those who mourn, for they shall be comforted."

Fasting is certainly not necessary to show sorrow for sin; nor should it be used to put on a show of spirituality. In fact, Jesus said that his disciples should be "careful not to do your 'acts of righteousness' before men, to be seen by them" (Matt. 6:1). If a person only wants to impress others by his outward show of piety, then he already has his reward. This is not what God is looking for.

Our desire is to be wise about good and innocent about evil. How can fasting help us in this endeavor? Ronnie W. Floyd mentions five disciplines that may help the Christian in living the Christian life:

Discipline 1: Fast from judging others; feast on Christ dwelling in them.

Discipline 2: Fast from fear of illness; feast on the healing power of God.

Discipline 3:   Fast from words that pollute; feast on speech that purifies.
Discipline 4:   Fast from discontent; feast on gratitude.
Discipline 5:   Fast from problems that overwhelm; feast on prayer that sustains.[50]

To many people, the only thing that comes to mind when fasting is mentioned is going without food. We see from the following passage that God desires much more for those who would be wise about good.

> "Shout it aloud, do not hold back. Raise your voice like a trumpet. Declare to my people their rebellion and to the house of Jacob their sins.
>
> For day after day they seek me out; they seem eager to know my ways, as if they were a nation that does what is right and has not forsaken the commands of its God. They ask me for just decisions and seem eager for God to come near them.
>
> 'Why have we fasted,' they say, 'and you have not seen it? Why have we humbled ourselves, and you have not noticed?' "Yet on the day of your fasting, you do as you please and exploit all your workers.
>
> Your fasting ends in quarreling and strife, and in striking each other with wicked fists. You cannot fast as you do today and expect your voice to be heard on high.
>
> Is this the kind of fast I have chosen, only a day for a man to humble himself? Is it only for bowing one's head like a reed and for lying on sackcloth and ashes? Is that what you call a fast, a day acceptable to the LORD?

Is not this the kind of fasting I have chosen: to loose the chains of injustice and untie the cords of the yoke, to set the oppressed free and break every yoke?

Is it not to share your food with the hungry and to provide the poor wanderer with shelter—when you see the naked, to clothe him, and not to turn away from your own flesh and blood?

Then your light will break forth like the dawn, and your healing will quickly appear; then your righteousness will go before you, and the glory of the LORD will be your rear guard." (Isa. 58:1–8)

Zechariah 7:5 raises an important question in approaching the subject of fasting: "Ask all the people of the land and the priests, 'When you fasted and mourned in the fifth and seventh months for the past seventy years, was it really for me that you fasted?'"

Fasting can be a very effective means of seeking God and His will. Though each person should certainly make sure not to do anything that could cause physical harm (as many exercise programs state, "consult your physician"), it should be noted that fasting does not necessarily include only doing without food. It can also be going without anything meaningful for a period of time to draw closer to God. It could be called a form of fasting that Paul referred to in 1 Corinthians 7:5 when he told husbands and wives not to "deprive each other except by mutual consent and for a time, so that you may devote yourselves to prayer." Fasting should never be a show or an attempt to impress either God or man. In Acts 13:2 the prophets and teachers in Antioch were together and they were "worshipping the Lord and fasting."

Though fasting is not commanded anywhere in the New Testament, that doesn't mean that it has no value for assisting God's children as they strive to draw closer to Him. If used wisely it can certainly be beneficial in helping us to focus on the things that are important to God.

Praising

Being truly wise about good means that the disciple is walking in God's will. When the Bible makes statements that say something to the effect of "this is God's will for you," the wise person will pay close attention. We see this statement: "Give thanks in all circumstances, for this is God's will for you in Christ Jesus" (1 Thess. 5:17). It is God's will that the followers of Christ give thank in all circumstances. Notice it says *all*. When life gets rough and everything seems to be going wrong, it takes a lot of faith to praise God; yet that is what He desires.

Praise is also a powerful weapon that can assist in being innocent about evil. When the believer focuses on God, he is not focusing on sin. Praise is such a powerful force in confronting our enemy that Jack Taylor calls it the believer's "chief weapon against the enemy."[51] As he discusses Jehoshaphat and the way he overcame the Moabites (2 Chron. 20:1–29), Taylor also describes the process of victory:

1) Jehoshaphat started at the point of the problem.
2) He stopped trusting in the flesh.
3) He concentrated on God.
4) He continued before God.
5) He confessed the truth of God.
6) He was committed to obeying God.
7) They collected riches from the crisis.[52]

The context of 2 Chronicles shows that Moab and others are attacking Israel; so Jehoshaphat and the children of Israel cry out to God for help. God tells them He is going to fight the battle for them and that they will not have to fight in this one. Jehoshaphat assigns "singers" to go out in front of the army to sing praise, and when they start, God ambushes the enemy for them.

Praise as a weapon in spiritual warfare is something that Satan has no answer for.[53] The Christian would be wise to have it as an active part of his arsenal for fighting the enemy.

Serving

If a disciple wants to be really wise about good, he needs to consider the lifestyle that God wants him to live. Look at what Jesus says in the following passage about the final judgment scene:

> When the Son of Man comes in his glory, and all the angels with him, he will sit on his throne in heavenly glory. All the nations will be gathered before him, and he will separate the people one from another as a shepherd separates the sheep from the goats. He will put the sheep on his right and the goats on his left.
>
> Then the King will say to those on his right, "Come, you who are blessed by my Father; take your inheritance, the kingdom prepared for you since the creation of the world. For I was hungry and you gave me something to eat, I was thirsty and you gave me something to drink, I was a stranger and you invited me in, I needed clothes and you clothed me, I was sick and you looked after me, I was in prison and you came to visit me."
>
> Then the righteous will answer him, "Lord, when did we see you hungry and feed you, or thirsty and give you something to drink? When did we see you a stranger and invite you in, or needing clothes and clothe you? When did we see you sick or in prison and got to visit you?"
>
> The King will reply, "I tell you the truth, whatever you did for one of the least of these brothers of mine, you did for me."

Then he will say to those on his left, "Depart from me, you who are cursed, into the eternal fire prepared for the devil and his angels. For I was hungry and you gave me nothing to eat, I was thirsty and you gave me nothing to drink, I was a stranger and you did not invite me in, I needed clothes and you did not clothe me, I was sick and in prison and you did not look after me."

They also will answer, "Lord, when did we see you hungry or thirsty or a stranger or needing clothes or sick or in prison, and did not help you?"

He will reply, "I tell you the truth, whatever you did not do for one of the least of these, you did not do for me."

Then they will go away to eternal punishment, but the righteous to eternal life. (Matt. 25: 31–46)

Even though this is a fairly lengthy passage, the message is still very clear: God wants people to serve others! In fact, Jesus said that when His followers minister to others, they are ministering to Him (Matt. 25:40).

Jesus set the example for the life He desires when he got down on hands and knees and washed the feet of His disciples (John 13:2–17). Jesus even washed the feet of His betrayer. Developing a servant's heart means that the disciple is becoming more like Christ, which is truly being wise about good.

Forgiving

The willingness to forgive is a vital issue for the believer. Jesus stated it this way: "When you stand praying, if you hold anything against anyone, forgive him, so that your Father in heaven may forgive you your sins" (Mark 11:25). In other words, if a person will not forgive, then he will not be forgiven. We have examples of both Jesus and Stephen offering forgiveness to those who were in the act of killing them. (Luke 23:34; Acts 7:60). This type of spirit is certainly not the natural response to others. It would be more natural if they had retaliated instead, but God desires far better from His children. Forgiving others is not always easy, but it is the will of God (Mark 11:25).

We've examined the subjects of fasting, praising, serving, and forgiving today. Each of these exercises can help the believer to grow closer to God and can enable the disciple to become wise about good.

Tomorrow we will examine the importance of who you associate with.

Food for thought:

- Fasting, praising, serving, forgiving. We could add other things to this list, but these show us some of the marvelous tools that God has provided for us to strengthen our resolve to serve and to know Him better. They also help us in cultivating both our relationship with God and with other people.
- Think about whether the time is appropriate for any of these disciplines. Is there a reason to spend time in prayer and fasting? We should always be spending time in praise. Serving and forgiving need to be ongoing parts of our daily lives.
- Pray for God to show you how to take the truths that we've examined today and to apply them so that you can get the most benefit possible.
- Especially on the topic of forgiving, please remember that if there is anyone you are unwilling to forgive, God won't forgive you either (Mark 11:25–26). Forgiveness is a vital topic when it comes to your relationship with God.

Day Thirty-two

Association

My son, if sinners entice you, do not give in to them. If they say, "Come along with us; let's lie in wait for someone's blood, let's waylay some harmless soul; let's swallow them alive, like the grave, and whole, like those who go down to the pit; we will get all sorts of valuable things and fill our houses with plunder; throw in your lot with us, and we will share a common purse"—my son, do not go along with them, do not set foot on their paths; for their feet rush into sin, they are swift to shed blood. How useless to spread a net in full view of all the birds! These men lie in wait for their own blood; they waylay only themselves! Such is the end of all who go after ill-gotten gain; it takes away the lives of those who get it. (Prov. 1:10–19)

Blessed is the man who does not walk in the counsel of the wicked or stand in the way of sinners or sit in the seat of mockers. (Ps. 1:1)

These passages are telling us in very plain language that the people we choose to associate with on a regular basis will have an impact on our lives. Lester Sumrall had this to say in his book on overcoming compulsive desires: "We need to be careful about who we choose as our close friends. This is why alcoholics and drug addicts usually need to break off old friendships and find new ones." Those old friendships make it virtually impossible for the addict to develop new, pure habits in life.[54]

To be able to return to innocence, the passage above tells us, we must stop maintaining close association with people who will lead us away from Christ.

Look at the words of Solomon in the following verse: "He who walks with the wise grows wise, but a companion of fools suffers harm" (Prov. 13:20). For the disciple to be wise about good, he needs to cultivate relationships with people who are already knowledgeable about godly living. LeRoy Eims in his book, *What Every Christian Should Know About Growing,* said that if a person wants to get some good advice about how to make a million dollars, he should not go to a beggar for this advice. He should go instead to someone who has already done it. He then went on to say that the same thing is true when a person wants advice about overcoming sin; he should go to someone who has successfully accomplished that feat, namely Jesus.[55]

As we study the habits of the early church we learn that believers spent a great deal of time associating with other Christians. In the fact the early Christians

> devoted themselves to the apostles' teaching and to the fellowship, to the breaking of bread and to prayer. Everyone was filled with awe, and many wonders and miraculous signs were done by the apostles. All the believers were together and had everything in common. Selling their possessions and goods, they gave to anyone as he had need. Every day they continued to meet together in the temple courts. They broke bread in their homes and ate together with glad and sincere hearts, praising God and enjoying the favor of all the people. (Acts 2:42–47)

They devoted themselves to fellowship (Acts 2:42). They met together every day. (2:46). When the writer of the Hebrew letter addressed the early saints, he admonished them with these words: "And let us consider how we may spur one another on toward love and good deeds. Let us not give up meeting together, as some are in the habit of doing, but let us encourage one another—and all the more as you see the Day approaching" (Heb. 10:24–25).

Since evil companions do corrupt (1 Cor. 15:33) and walking with the wise makes a man wiser (Prov. 13:20), the best advice for a person who wants to be wise about good is to associate with people who will draw him closer to God.

Food for thought:

- Who do you spend your time with socially?
- Are they helping you in your relationship with God?
- Can you lift up the name of Jesus while you're with them without feeling like you're going to be rejected?
- As you answer these questions, please remember that bad companions do corrupt good morals (1 Cor. 15:33).
- Try to choose friends and spend time with people who will help you to draw closer to the Lord.
- If you discover that you have friends who are keeping you from an intimate walk with God, please ask Him to give you the wisdom, the strength, and the love that you need to deal with the situation in a Christ-like manner.

Putting on Your Armor

Day Thirty-three

The Breastplate of Righteousness

Our key text for the next few days is going to be Ephesians 6:10–18. Here's what Paul wrote in that passage:

> Finally, be strong in the Lord and in his mighty power. Put on the full armor of God so that you can take your stand against the devil's schemes. For our struggle is not against flesh and blood, but against the rulers, against the authorities, against the powers of this dark world and against the spiritual forces of evil in the heavenly realms. Therefore put on the full armor of God, so that when the day of evil comes, you may be able to stand your ground, and after you have done everything, to stand. Stand firm then, with the belt of truth buckled around your waist, with the breastplate of righteousness in place, and with your feet fitted with the readiness that comes from the gospel of peace. In addition to all this, take up the shield of faith, with which you can extinguish all the flaming arrows of the evil one. Take the helmet of salvation and the sword of the Spirit, which is the word of

God. And pray in the Spirit on all occasions with all kinds of prayers and requests. With this in mind, be alert and always keep on praying for all the saints.

Before we start examining the various parts of the armor that God has provided for our defense, I think it's important for us to note who God says we are fighting against. Our battle is not against flesh and blood! Your spouse is not your enemy. Your children or your parents are not your enemy. Your boss is not your enemy. We often get side-tracked into believing that the person we seem to be having a problem with at the moment is our real enemy—that's a lie. It's a distraction. The real enemy is not flesh and blood. The real battle is against "the rulers, against the authorities, against the powers of this dark world and against the spiritual forces of evil in the heavenly realms." The battle is against real spiritual forces who want to destroy you in order to bring harm to God. But God has provided armor to enable us to be victorious. Because the enemy is real and the stakes are high, make the commitment to always keep all of your armor on, so that God can be glorified and you won't become an unnecessary casualty on the battle field because of negligence in keeping your armor in place.

Today we are going to consider the importance of putting on the breastplate of righteousness.

Righteousness

Jesus said in the Sermon on the Mount that those who hunger and thirst for righteousness would be satisfied (Matt. 5:6). What does it mean to be hungry or thirsty? We understand physical hunger and physical thirst, but Jesus says that there is a special blessedness reserved for those who hunger and thirst for righteousness, cultivating that burning desire never to settle for anything less than genuine righteousness. In Matthew 6:1 He warned people not to fall into the trap of trying to do righteous things in order to impress others. Righteous living is not about trying to show others how good or holy you are. In fact, if you give in to the desire to impress people, you have already received your reward. Our sights need to be set much higher. We should be seeking to do the things we do in order to bring glory to our creator. He made us; He provides for us; and He has plans for spending all of eternity with us. What people think should pale in comparison with living to please Him and draw others to Him.

In Matthew 6:33 Jesus said that instead of worrying we should seek first God's kingdom and His righteousness and then God would see to it that our needs are taken care of. So often we get our priorities out of line. We spend most of our lives planning for our retirement and worrying about our bills and our vacations and where we will send the kids to school. Though we are certainly commanded to be good stewards of what God gives us, and He does expect us to plan wisely and use what He has given us in a wise manner, we often spend so much time dwelling on those things that we completely leave out the important matters. Seek God's reign in your life first. Seek the righteousness that He wants you to have as a priority. Our daily necessities are less important than these. The truth is that God already knows you have needs and He is more than able to provide for those needs, but His greatest desire is to have an intimate walk with His children.

Look at what the Hebrew writer says in the following passage:

We have much to say about this, but it is hard to explain because you are slow to learn. In fact, though by this time you ought to be teachers, you need someone to teach you the elementary truths of God's word all over again. You need milk, not solid food! Anyone who lives on milk, being still an infant, is not acquainted with the teaching about righteousness. But solid food is for the mature, who by constant use have trained themselves to distinguish good from evil.

> Therefore let us leave the elementary teachings about Christ and go on to maturity. (Heb. 5:11–6:1)

A lot of people in churches today are living the same way the people were living when this letter was written. Even though they had been "church members" for years, they were still living on a diet of milk. That hadn't moved on to meat. They didn't understand that righteousness is a maturity issue. This whole book is about learning to live righteously before our God, being wise about what is good and innocent about what is evil (Rom. 16:19). That's another way of describing what it means to live a righteous life. Cultivating passion for being pure.

Paul told the church in Rome that the kingdom of God was about righteousness, peace, and joy in the Holy Spirit (Rom. 14:17). How often do we lose sight of the things that really matter? Righteousness, peace, and joy in the Holy Spirit. How important are those things to you in your daily walk with Christ? For most of us, if we are really honest, they aren't really important are they? It's time we get serious about the things of God and ask for His help in getting our priorities in line with His. Look at what Paul wrote to the church in Corinth:

> Now if the ministry that brought death, which was engraved in letters on stone, came with glory, so that the Israelites could not look steadily at the face of Moses because of its glory, fading though it was, will not the ministry of the Spirit be even more glorious? If the ministry that condemns men is glorious, how much more glorious is the ministry that brings righteousness! For what was glorious has no glory now in comparison with the surpassing glory. And if what was fading away came with glory, how much greater is the glory of that which lasts! (2 Cor. 3:7–11)

The ministry of the Spirit brings righteousness. That ministry is one that lasts. It is a ministry that has an ever increasing glory. In fact the purpose of that ministry is to help mold you to be transformed into the likeness of Christ (2 Cor. 3:18). But God cannot complete the work of transforming us if we are constantly fighting Him and resisting the changes that He desires to make. If we choose to live our lives in an unrighteous or unholy way, He will allow us to follow that path and we should not be surprised when we do not grow to be more like Jesus. Paul told the church in Galatia that people will always reap what they sow. If you sow to please the flesh, you will reap destruction, but if you sow to the Spirit, you will reap the benefits of that, leading to holiness and eternal life (Gal. 6:7–8).

I think it is important to note here that Paul warns against any attempts that people may make to try to gain their righteousness or their salvation based on following law. No one is saved by observing law. Never have been and never will be. So don't try. (See Gal. 2:21).

The breastplate of righteousness is a wonderful blessing. Though righteousness is credited to our account as the result of our faith (Rom. 4), we are also commanded to grow in righteousness. So, as we've seen in many other areas, there is the righteousness that God provides and the righteousness that He commands. Those who are growing to maturity understand that righteousness is vital to our spiritual health. Maturity has, through constant practice, trained the senses to discern between what is good and what is evil (Heb. 5:14). If you haven't already done this, please commit to pressing on to maturity. God wants so much for you to be mature, complete, and strong. Don't settle for anything less.

Food for thought:

- Do you hunger and thirst for the righteousness of God?
- Is His kingdom (His reign) a priority in your life?
- Are there unrighteous areas that you have allowed to be a part of your life? If so, what do you plan to do to change that?
- Are you committed to pressing on to maturity? If so, that means growing in your understanding of what righteous living is really about (according to God).
- Spend some time praying for God to show you more ways that you can be holy and righteous (not in an attempt to please or impress people, but to grow in your relationship with Him).

Day Thirty-four

The Belt of Truth

Truth. So often in the world today if you want to discuss truth—especially spiritual truth—people will frequently throw out statements like "Well, that's your truth." So I think it's important as we enter into a discussion of truth to start by asking, Is truth subjective?

In many areas of life it is easy to see that there is only one correct answer to a question. In measuring distance it is easy to see where accuracy becomes crucial. Can you imagine the fights that would start if the people designing a race track decided that using the correct measurements didn't really matter? Suppose they designed the lanes but when you checked them, the inside lanes were actually several meters closer to the finish line than the outside lanes. So on the 100-meter dash the person in lane one would run only 90 meters and the person on the outside would do the full 100. Unless you're the runner in lane one, the distance matters. It certainly matters in sports. It also matters in math. In math two plus two equals four. We can argue all we want and say that two plus two equals seven, but it doesn't change the facts. We can easily see where there are many areas where the truth is not subjective. Spiritually the same thing is true. There may be some areas where there is a certain degree of uncertainty, but some things are either true or they are not. God either exists or He doesn't. Whether someone believes in Him or not does not change the truth.

We are going to spend the next few minutes examining what the Bible reveals about the truth and how putting on the belt of truth provides a wonderful blessing to our lives.

> In the beginning was the Word, and the Word was with God, and the Word was God. He was with God in the beginning.

> Through him all things were made; without him nothing was made that has been made. (John 1:1–3)

> The Word became flesh and made his dwelling among us. We have seen his glory, the glory of the One and Only, who came from the Father, full of grace and truth. (John 1:14)

> For the law was given through Moses; grace and truth came through Jesus Christ. (John 1:17)

> Jesus answered, "I am the way and the truth and the life. No one comes to the Father except through me." (John 14:6)

Some extremely important truths are revealed in the passages listed above. These are foundational issues for Christians. Jesus is God. He is the creator. He became flesh and lived among us. He brought both grace and truth. He is the way. He is the truth! He is the life. And He is the only way to get to the Father! Though there are certainly many ways that people in the world claim that they can get to God, Jesus did not allow for that. If He is who He claimed to be (and all of the evidence proves that He is), then no one comes to the Father except through Him.

There is a battle going on in the world between truth and lies (see more on Day Seven). That same battle is being fought in your mind. You are either listening to the truth or you are believing the lies. Let the truths in the following passages really sink in.

> Jesus said, "If you hold to my teaching, you are really my disciples. Then you will know the truth, and the truth will set you free." (John 8:31–32)

> Paul, a servant of God and an apostle of Jesus Christ for the faith of God's elect and the knowledge of the truth that leads to godliness. (Titus 1:1)

> This is the message we have heard from him and declare to you: God is light; in him there is no darkness at all. If we claim to have fellowship with him yet walk in the darkness, we lie and do not live by the truth. But if we walk in the light, as he is in the light, we have fellowship with one another, and the blood of Jesus, his Son, purifies us from all sin.
>
> If we claim to be without sin, we deceive ourselves and the truth is not in us. If we confess our sins, he is faithful and just and will forgive us our sins and purify us from all unrighteousness. If we claim we have not sinned, we make him out to be a liar and his word has no place in our lives. (1 John 1:5–10)

Jesus said that if we would hold to His teachings, we would know the truth and the truth would set us free. Freedom. What a blessing. Free from guilt and shame. Free from law. Free from the law of sin and death. The truth will set you free! But it begins with holding to the teaching of Christ.

Paul said that knowledge of the truth leads to godliness. And then John reveals to us that the truth is not in us if we are believing lies and refusing to see life as it really is. Yes, there will be times that we are weak and we will sin. Don't deceive yourself into thinking that you're perfect. Recognize the truth. When you do sin (this is not a license to sin, but a recognition of our weaknesses), confess it to God and He will forgive you!

Put on the belt of truth (Eph. 6:14). Consider what Jesus revealed about truth. He said "I am the . . . truth" (John 14:6). Clothe yourself with Christ. Hold to His teaching. Live your life focusing on the truth and exposing the lies. Walking in Christ means walking in freedom. "If you hold to my teaching, . . . you will know the truth and the truth will set you free" (John 8:31–32).

Food for thought:

- What changes do you need to make in order to live your life based on truth? What lies have you been holding on to?
- What do you think the freedom that Jesus promised is all about?
- Challenge for today: Read Ephesians 4:15 and ask yourself what changes in your speech need to take place for you to consistently speak the truth in love.

Day Thirty-five

The Gospel of Peace and the Helmet of Salvation

The gospel is the good news of peace (Eph. 6:15). Always be prepared to share the good news of peace. We are surrounded by people who have no good news and no peace in their lives, and yet the message of the cross is that God loves them and desires a relationship with them so much that He was willing to die so that He would not have to spend eternity without them. We need to be letting the world know that peace is available. Not necessarily the absence of war, but on a much more personal level. God offers people peace within.

Today we are going to examine both the gospel of peace and the helmet of salvation. They are so closely related that I don't think we can adequately discuss one without dealing with the other.

The Gospel

> I am not ashamed of the gospel, because it is the power of God for the salvation of everyone who believes: first for the Jew, then for the Gentile. For in the gospel a righteousness from God is revealed, a righteousness that is by faith from first to last, just as it is written: "The righteous will live by faith." (Rom. 1:16–17)

> Now, brothers, I want to remind you of the gospel I preached to you, which you received and on which you have taken your stand. By this gospel you are saved, if you hold firmly to the word I preached to you. Otherwise, you have believed in vain.

> For what I received I passed on to you as of first importance: that Christ died for our sins according to the Scriptures, that he was buried, that he was raised on the third day according to the Scriptures." (1 Cor. 15:1–4)

The gospel is the power of God for salvation. Paul said that the gospel is the death, burial, and the resurrection of Jesus. That is the good news! It is the heart of the salvation message and it is the power of God in the resurrection that offers hope to our lives as well. The message of peace that we offer to people is based on the power revealed in the death, burial, and the resurrection of Christ. He died to free us from sin as well as to free us from our fear of death. Listen to what Hebrews 2:14–15 reveals to us:

> Since the children have flesh and blood, he too shared in their humanity so that by his death he might destroy him who holds the power of death—that is, the devil—and free those who all their lives were held in slavery by their fear of death.

In the resurrection Jesus destroyed the one who holds the power of death—the devil—and at the same time freed those who spent their entire lives being held in slavery by the fear of death. Look at the glorious power and grace that God revealed here. The most devastating weapon that our enemy has, and God disarmed him in one glorious act. By dying for us and coming back to life, He shows us that we have nothing to fear.

The gospel message is defined as the death, burial, and the resurrection of Jesus. So the question is often raised, What must I do to be saved?

What I want to do here is to look at how that question was answered in the New Testament and to look at some examples of what people did when they were confronted with the gospel message.

The Helmet of Salvation

> Take the helmet of salvation. (Eph. 6:17)

> All have sinned and fall short of the glory of God. (Rom. 3:23)

Just as Moses lifted up the snake in the desert, so the Son of Man must be lifted up, that everyone who believes in him may have eternal life.

For God so loved the world that he gave his one and only Son, that whoever believes in him shall not perish but have eternal life. For God did not send his Son into the world to condemn the world, but to save the world through him. Whoever believes in him is not condemned, but whoever does not believe stands condemned already because he has not believed in the name of God's one and only Son. (John 3:14–18)

But what does it say? "The word is near you; it is in your mouth and in your heart," that is, the word of faith we are proclaiming: That if you confess with your mouth, "Jesus is Lord," and believe in your heart that God raised him from the dead, you will be saved. For it is with your heart that you believe and are justified, and it is with your mouth that you confess and are saved. As the Scripture says, "Anyone who trusts in him will never be put to shame. (Rom 10:8–11)

"Therefore let all Israel be assured of this: God has made this Jesus, whom you crucified, both Lord and Christ."

When the people heard this, they were cut to the heart and said to Peter and the other apostles, "Brothers, what shall we do?"

Peter replied, "Repent and be baptized, every one of you, in the name of Jesus Christ for the forgiveness of your sins. And you will receive the gift of the Holy Spirit. The promise is for you and your children and for all who are far off—for all whom the Lord our God will call." (Acts 2:36–39)

About midnight Paul and Silas were praying and singing hymns to God, and the other prisoners were listening to them. Suddenly there was such a violent earthquake that the foundations of the prison were shaken. At once all the prison doors flew open, and everybody's chains came loose. The jailer woke up, and when he saw the prison doors open, he drew his sword and was about to kill himself because he thought the prisoners had escaped. But Paul shouted, "Don't harm yourself! We are all here!"

The jailer called for lights, rushed in and fell trembling before Paul and Silas. He then brought them out and asked, "Sirs, what must I do to be saved?"

They replied, "Believe in the Lord Jesus, and you will be saved—you and your household." Then they spoke the word of the Lord to him and to all the others in his house. At that hour of the night the jailer took them and washed their wounds; then immediately he and all his family were baptized. (Acts 16:25–33).

For it is by grace you have been saved, through faith—and this not from yourselves, it is the gift of God—not by works, so that no one can boast. For we are God's workmanship, created in Christ Jesus to do good works, which God prepared in advance for us to do. (Eph. 2:8–10)

You are all sons of God through faith in Christ Jesus, for all of you who were baptized into Christ have clothed yourselves with Christ. (Gal. 3:26–27)

We died to sin; how can we live in it any longer? Or don't you know that all of us who were baptized into Christ Jesus were baptized into his death? We were therefore buried with him through baptism into death in order that, just as Christ was raised from the dead through the glory of the Father, we too may live a new life. (Rom. 6:2–4)

For Christ died for sins once for all, the righteous for the unrighteous, to bring you to God. He was put to death in the body but made alive by the Spirit, through whom also he went and preached to the spirits in prison who disobeyed long ago when God waited patiently in the days of Noah while the ark was being built. In it only a few people, eight in all, were saved through water, and this water symbolizes baptism that now saves you also—not the removal of dirt from the body but the pledge of a good conscience toward God. It saves you by the resurrection of Jesus Christ. (1 Peter 3:18–21)

Speak and act as those who are going to be judged by the law that gives freedom, because judgment without mercy will be shown to anyone who has not been merciful. Mercy triumphs over judgment!

What good is it, my brothers, if a man claims to have faith but has no deeds? Can such faith save him? Suppose a brother or sister is without clothes and daily food. If one of you says to him, "Go, I wish you well; keep warm and well fed," but does nothing about his physical needs, what good is it? In the same way, faith by itself, if it is not accompanied by action, is dead.

But someone will say, "You have faith; I have deeds."

Show me your faith without deeds, and I will show you my faith by what I do. You believe that there is one God. Good! Even the demons believe that—and shudder.

You foolish man, do you want evidence that faith without deeds is useless? Was not our ancestor Abraham considered righteous for what he did when he offered his son Isaac on the altar? You see that his faith and his actions were working together, and his faith was made complete by what he did. And the scripture was fulfilled that says, "Abraham believed God, and it was credited to him as righteousness," and he was called God's friend. You see that a person is justified by what he does and not by faith alone.

In the same way, was not even Rahab the prostitute considered righteous for what she did when she gave lodging to the spies and sent them off in a different direction? As the body without the spirit is dead, so faith without deeds is dead. (James 2:12–25)

We have looked at a lot of different passages here, but I want to make sure that everything is very clear. We are saved through faith. But the Bible is very clear that genuine faith always includes obedience. Faith is not simple lip service. Faith without works is dead. No one will ever be saved through works. It is foolish to even try. But biblical faith always acts. In Acts chapter two, Peter's listeners were pierced in their hearts. They believed that what Peter was telling them was true (they had crucified the Son of God), and they cried out, "What shall we do?" Peter's answer: Repent, and be baptized in the name of Jesus for the forgiveness of your sins and you will receive the gift of the Holy Spirit. Now that you have come to believe, you need to turn away from your sins. You need to be baptized into Christ. When you do that, here is what God will do. He will forgive your sins and He will place His Spirit inside you to enable you to live the new life you are starting.

Faith saves! But faith without obedience is not genuine faith. Although the demons in James chapter two "believe and shudder," they are still not saved. We likewise are not saved because we mentally accept the truth, but because we act on that faith and demonstrate that it is genuine. We are not in any way saved by works, we work (obey) because we believe.

I want to look at one more example that I think is extremely important to illustrate the process. Let's look at the conversion of Saul (Paul).

> Then Paul said: "I am a Jew, born in Tarsus of Cilicia, but brought up in this city. Under Gamaliel I was thoroughly trained in the law of our fathers and was just as zealous for God as any of you are today. I persecuted the followers of this Way to their death, arresting both men and women and throwing them into prison, as also the high priest and all the Council can testify. I even obtained letters from them to their brothers in Damascus, and went there to bring these people as prisoners to Jerusalem to be punished.

"About noon as I came near Damascus, suddenly a bright light from heaven flashed around me. I fell to the ground and heard a voice say to me, 'Saul! Saul! Why do you persecute me?'

"'Who are you, Lord?' I asked.

"'I am Jesus of Nazareth, whom you are persecuting,' he replied. My companions saw the light, but they did not understand the voice of him who was speaking to me.

"'What shall I do, Lord?' I asked.

"'Get up,' the Lord said, 'and go into Damascus. There you will be told all that you have been assigned to do.' My companions led me by the hand into Damascus, because the brilliance of the light had blinded me.

"A man named Ananias came to see me. He was a devout observer of the law and highly respected by all the Jews living there. He stood beside me and said, 'Brother Saul, receive your sight!' And at that very moment I was able to see him.

"Then he said: 'The God of our fathers has chosen you to know his will and to see the Righteous One and to hear words from his mouth. You will be his witness to all men of what you have seen and heard. And now what are you waiting for? Get up, be baptized and wash your sins away, calling on his name." (Acts 22:3–16)

Saul actually talked with Jesus on the road to Damascus, and yet three days later when Ananias came to him he was told that what he needed to do was to get up and be baptized *so that his sins could be washed away.*

We are saved because of our faith. We demonstrate the validity of our faith by obeying what God has commanded. He commanded us to believe and be baptized into Christ so that He can forgive us our sins and place His Spirit inside us. In giving the great commission to His disciples He said,

> "All authority in heaven and on earth has been given to me. Therefore go and make disciples of all nations, baptizing them in the name of the Father and of the Son and of the Holy Spirit, and teaching them to obey everything I have commanded you. And surely I am with you always, to the very end of the age." (Matt. 28:18–20)

The gospel is the death, burial, and the resurrection of Jesus. We are saved by the grace of God and through faith in Christ. We prove that faith when we are united with Christ in His death, buried with Him in baptism and raised to live a new life. Then we are commissioned to go and make disciples of all nations.

The gospel brings peace to people's lives. Salvation offers hope. Jesus died to deliver us from the bondage of sin and to offer hope for life. Make sure you are always prepared with the gospel of peace and that you are indeed saved. Remember—Jesus said "I am the way, the truth, and the life, no one comes to the Father except through me" (John 14:6). He is the only way that we can be saved.

Food for thought:

- How does James tell us that we prove that we really do believe?
- Can faith by itself (without obedience) save you?
- How does God's grace affect the way you live your life?
- What is the core message of the gospel?
- What does baptism represent?
- Are you saved? If not, what are you going to do about it?

Day Thirty-six

The Shield of Faith

"In addition to all this, take up the shield of faith, with which you can extinguish all the flaming arrows of the evil one" (Eph. 6:16). Through faith we can extinguish every flaming arrow the enemy throws at us. What an amazing truth. Remember that our battle is against the spiritual forces of evil who want to destroy us, but when our armor is in place and we live by faith, we do not have to be defeated. Isn't God wonderful? He helps us to see that there is an enemy who wants to do us harm, and then He provides every piece of armor we need to be able to stand up against that enemy and live victorious lives. So why are so many Christians consistently being defeated? Because they are not putting on the full armor.

Today we will be looking at what it means to live by faith.

It was not through law that Abraham and his offspring received the promise that he would be heir of the world, but through the righteousness that comes by faith. For if those who live by law are heirs, faith has no value and the promise is worthless, because law brings wrath. And where there is no law there is no transgression.

Therefore, the promise comes by faith, so that it may be by grace and may be guaranteed to all Abraham's offspring—not only to those who are of the law but also to those who are of the faith of Abraham. He is the father of us all. As it is written: "I have made you a father of many nations." He is our father in the sight of God, in whom he believed—the God who gives life to the dead and calls things that are not as though they were.

Against all hope, Abraham in hope believed and so became the father of many nations, just as it had been said to him, "So shall your offspring be." Without weakening in his faith, he faced the fact that his body was as good as dead—since he was about a hundred years old—and that Sarah's womb was also dead. Yet he did not waver through unbelief regarding the promise of God, but was strengthened in his faith and gave glory to God, being fully persuaded that God had power to do what he had promised. This is why "it was credited to him as righteousness." The words "it was credited to him" were written not for him alone, but also for us, to whom God will credit righteousness—for us who believe in him who raised Jesus our Lord from the dead. He was delivered over to death for our sins and was raised to life for our justification. (Rom. 4:13–25)

How do we obtain faith? Faith comes through hearing the word of God (Rom. 10:17). As we study God's Word and begin to live by it, He begins to transform and give us the guidance that we need. (We will look at this concept more tomorrow when we look utilizing the sword of the Spirit.) This is where James's admonition to be "doers and not just hearers" is critical (James 1:22).

You who are trying to be justified by law have been alienated from Christ; you have fallen away from grace. But by faith we eagerly await through the Spirit the righteousness for which we hope. For in Christ Jesus neither circumcision nor uncircumcision has any value. The only thing that counts is faith expressing itself through love. (Gal. 5:4–6)

Living by faith. This is not something that God says is a neat idea if you are a believer. He says that without it you're not really saved. "Without faith it is impossible to please God" (Heb. 11:6). The righteous will live by faith (Rom. 1:17; Gal. 3:11).

So, what is faith? "Now faith is being sure of what we hope for and certain of what we do not see" (Heb. 11:1). Faith is the evidence or the assurance that what we hope for is going to come to pass and it is the certainty that the object of our hope will come to pass. Faith is not wishful thinking. It takes the evidence and says that because of that evidence we can be sure that God will keep His promises. Look at prophecies that have been fulfilled concerning Christ. Something like three hundred and thirty different prophecies were written anywhere from 1400 years to 500 years before He came and every one of them came true, to the letter: of the line of Abraham, Isaac, and Jacob; of the line of David; born in Bethlehem; born of a virgin; escape to Egypt; ministry in Galilee; entering Jerusalem riding on a donkey; rejected by His own people; killed with criminals; buried in a rich man's tomb; raised from the dead. These are only a few of the prophecies given, and every single one of them came true. The evidence leaves room for no other conclusion than that He is the Messiah and the Savior of the world.

So, on a practical level in our lives today, what still counts is faith expressing itself in love (Gal. 5:6). As we go through life and begin living by faith and not by sight (2 Cor. 5:7) we begin to see that there is a much bigger picture than merely existing. God desires to accomplish so much more in us and through us than we often want to admit or possibly allow. But He demands that we live each day by faith. That doesn't mean that we in any way fail to take care of our responsibilities (1 Tim. 5:8). It does mean that our priorities will change. Our focus will be different. Paul said in Romans 14:23 that whatever we do that is not done in faith is sinful. So the standard, and the importance, of living by faith is very high. But the promise is also extremely impressive. Faith is the avenue through which we overcome the world (1 John 5:4). By using the shield of faith, we can extinguish every single arrow the evil one throws at us (Eph. 6:16). So the only real question is—are you living by faith?

Food for thought:

- Does knowing that the shield of faith can protect you from *every* attack the evil one throws change your perspective of how these spiritual battles play out in life?
- Isn't it great to know that no matter what the attack is, God has provided protection?
- What counts is faith expressing itself through love. How can you express your faith in a very loving way today?

Day Thirty-seven

The Sword of the Spirit

"Take the helmet of salvation and the sword of the Spirit, which is the word of God" (Eph. 6:17). Today we're going to spend some time examining exactly what this passage says. To really see everything that is meant here I think it's important to go back and examine the context.

> Finally, be strong in the Lord and in his mighty power. Put on the full armor of God so that you can take your stand against the devil's schemes. For our struggle is not against flesh and blood, but against the rulers, against the authorities, against the powers of this dark world and against the spiritual forces of evil in the heavenly realms. Therefore put on the full armor of God, so that when the day of evil comes, you may be able to stand your ground, and after you have done everything, to stand. Stand firm then, with the belt of truth buckled around your waist, with the breastplate of righteousness in place, and with your feet fitted with the readiness that comes from the gospel of peace. In addition to all this, take up the shield of faith, with which you can extinguish all the flaming arrows of the evil one. Take the helmet of salvation and the sword of the Spirit, which is the word of God. (Eph. 6:10–17)

Remember that the context is the spiritual battle that we are in. We are fighting against a spiritual enemy. And we are told to put on the full armor that God has provided. Make sure the belt of truth is in place; keep the breastplate of righteousness on at all times; always be ready to share the gospel of peace, keep the shield of faith up, make sure the helmet of salvation is in place; and effectively wield the sword of the Spirit, which is the word of God.

For a long time I misunderstood part of this verse. I think it will be beneficial for us to spend a minute or two looking at the original language. Two different words are used in the New Testament for "word." One of them is *logos*. This is the word used in John 1:1 "In the beginning was the Word [*logos*], and the Word [*logos*] was with God, and the Word [*logos*] was God." But in Ephesians six the word used is not *logos*, it is *rhema*. *Rhema* deals primarily with the spoken message rather than simply the message itself. This word is used seven times outside of Matthew, Mark, Luke, John, and Acts. I'm going to go show all seven times to help us see how it is used, and then we'll spend a little time looking at what this means to us.

> But what does it say? "The word [*rhema*] is near you; it is in your mouth and in your heart," that is, the word [*rhema*] of faith we are proclaiming. (Rom, 10:8)

> This will be my third visit to you. "Every matter must be established by the testimony [*rhema*] of two or three witnesses." (2 Cor. 13:1)

> Take the helmet of salvation and the sword of the Spirit, which is the word [*rhema*] of God. (Eph. 6:17)

> It is impossible for those who have once been enlightened, who have tasted the heavenly gift, who have shared in the Holy Spirit, who have tasted the goodness of the word [*rhema*] of God and the powers of the coming age, if they fall away, to be brought back to repentance, because to their loss they are crucifying the Son of God all over again and subjecting him to public disgrace. (Heb. 6:4–6)

> "All men are like grass, and all their glory is like the flowers of the field; the grass withers and the flowers fall, but the word [*rhema*] of the Lord stands forever." And this is the word [*rhema*] that was preached to you." (1 Peter 1:24–25)

So, how does speaking the word of God really help us? To really answer that accurately it will be beneficial to see how Jesus handled it. Look at Matthew 4:1–11.

> Then Jesus was led by the Spirit into the desert to be tempted by the devil. After fasting forty days and forty nights, he was hungry. The tempter came to him and said, "If you are the Son of God, tell these stones to become bread."
>
> Jesus answered, "It is written: 'Man does not live on bread alone, but on every word that comes from the mouth of God.'"
>
> Then the devil took him to the holy city and had him stand on the highest point of the temple. "If you are the Son of God," he said, "throw yourself down. For it is written:
>
> 'He will command his angels concerning you, and they will lift you up in their hands, so that you will not strike your foot against a stone.'"
>
> Jesus answered him, "It is also written: 'Do not put the Lord your God to the test.'
>
> Again, the devil took him to a very high mountain and showed him all the kingdoms of the world and their splendor. "All this I will give you," he said, "if you will bow down and worship me."
>
> Jesus said to him, "Away from me, Satan! For it is written: 'Worship the Lord your God, and serve him only.'"
>
> Then the devil left him, and angels came and attended him.

Jesus was being tempted. His response was to answer with the Word of God. There is a tremendous amount of wisdom in learning from His example. But to respond the way He did we need to recognize a couple of things. Jesus already knew what the Word of God said on the issues. He had hidden the Word in His heart (Ps. 119:11). He recognized when He was being tempted, and He responded with Scripture. When we respond to temptation by proclaiming what God says on the issue, we are wielding the *rhema* (the Word) of God. That is the sword which the Spirit can use to enable us to live victoriously.

Food for thought:

- Have you hidden the Word in your heart so that you are able to respond appropriately when you're faced with temptation?
- If it is out of the overflow of the heart that the mouth speaks (Matt. 12:34), what changes can you make to be sure that your heart is filled with the things of God?
- Let the awesome power of this truth sink in for a while: The same Spirit who inspired the writing of scripture is dwelling in you and in transforming you to be like Jesus. The Spirit is also the one who enables you to effectively use the word of God. Isn't God great? He knows how weak we are and He has provided everything we need to experience life and to become godly men and women (2 Peter 1:3).

Victory Is Here

Day Thirty-eight

You Will Never Stumble

Grace and peace be multiplied to you in the knowledge of God and of Jesus our Lord; seeing that His divine power has granted to us everything pertaining to life and godliness, through the true knowledge of Him who called us by His own glory and excellence. For by these He has granted to us His precious and magnificent promises, in order that by them you might become partakers of *the* divine nature, having escaped the corruption that is in the world by lust. Now for this very reason also, applying all diligence, in your faith supply moral excellence, and in *your* moral excellence, and in *your* knowledge; and in *your* knowledge, self-control, and in *your* self-control, perseverance, and in *your* perseverance, godliness; and in *your* godliness, brotherly kindness, and in *your* brotherly kindness, love. For if these *qualities* are yours and are increasing, they render you neither useless nor unfruitful in the true knowledge of our Lord Jesus Christ. For he who lacks these *qualities* is blind or shortsighted, having forgotten *his* purification from his former sins. Therefore, brethren, be all the more diligent to make certain about

His calling and choosing you; for as long as you practice these things, you will never stumble; for in this way the entrance into the eternal kingdom of our Lord and Savior Jesus Christ will be abundantly supplied to you. (2 Peter 1:2–11, NASB)

What a wonderful thing to know that God has given us a blueprint for success in knowing how to live so that we will never stumble. Peter starts the list of qualities mentioned above with the assumption that there is already faith present, so we will begin with that same assumption. We will examine each of the areas that a person should strive to add to faith.

Moral Excellence

The term "moral excellence" used in the NASB, is translated "goodness" in the NIV and "virtue" in the KJV. Peter is telling believers that there should be a sense of purity in their lives that is radically different from that of the world. Moral excellence describes the Christian's approach to morality. Mediocrity is not enough! Ethelbert Bullinger says that the Greek word *aretay* means "superiority" when speaking of God and then, "in a moral sense, that which gives man his worth, his efficiency, his moral excellence."[56] Christians should be morally excellent, not out of a desire to be better than someone else but because God is the standard and the desire is to be like Him.

Knowledge

"You stumble day and night, and the prophets stumble with you. So I will destroy your mother—my people are destroyed from lack of knowledge. Because you have rejected knowledge, I also reject you as my priests; because you have ignored the law of your God, I also will ignore your children." (Hosea 4:5–6)

> Knowledge puffs up, but love builds up. (1 Cor. 8:1)

> Paul, a servant of God and an apostle of Jesus Christ for the faith of God's elect and the knowledge of the truth that leads to godliness—a faith and knowledge resting on the hope of eternal life, which God, who does not lie, promised before the beginning of time, and at his appointed season he brought his word to light through the preaching entrusted to me by the command of God our Savior. (Tit. 1:1–3)

Knowledge simply for the sake of knowledge puffs up according to 1 Corinthians 8:1, but there is another level of knowledge that is imperative for God's people. Hosea said that the people of God "are destroyed for lack of knowledge" (Hosea 4:5–6). They had a lack of knowledge concerning God and His will for their lives. In Titus, Paul states that knowledge of the truth will lead to godliness (Titus 1:1). That is the kind of knowledge that this book is all about: seeking to know God and His will in order to be wise about good and innocent about evil.

Self-control

When Paul was preaching to Felix, his message was one of righteousness, self-control, and the judgment to come (Acts 24:25). In Galatians 5:22–23 we learn that self-control is listed as a fruit of the Spirit. Upon close examination we can see why God would consider self-control important in the life of a Christian. Look at the following passages:

> "Everything is permissible for me"—but not everything is beneficial. "Everything is permissible for me"—but I will not be mastered by anything. (1 Cor. 6:12)

> They promise them freedom, while they themselves are slaves of depravity—for a man is a slave to whatever has mastered him. (2 Pet. 2:19)

God wants His children to be in control at all times. This makes any kind of addiction or compulsive behavior a very important issue for the believer. Paul said, "I will not be mastered by anything" (1 Cor. 6:12). Peter said that anything that has mastered someone has made him its slave (2 Pet. 2:19). The disciple of Christ needs to carefully examine his life and if there is anything that has mastered him, whether it is sinful in and of itself or not, he needs to get control over it. God does not want His children to be mastered by anything but Him.

Perseverance

> Therefore, since we have been justified through faith we have peace with God through our Lord Jesus Christ, through whom we have gained access by faith into this grace in which we now stand. And we rejoice in the hope of the glory of God. Not only so, but we also rejoice in our sufferings, because we know that suffering produces perseverance; perseverance, character; and character, hope. And hope does not disappoint us, because God has poured out his love into our hearts by the Holy Spirit, whom he has given us. (Rom. 5:1–5)

> Consider it pure joy, my brothers, whenever you face trials of many kinds, because you know that the testing of your faith develops perseverance. Perseverance must finish its work so that you may be mature and complete, not lacking anything. (James 1:2–4)

The development of perseverance comes through pain and suffering, but it is an important part of the growth process. In both of the passages above we see that suffering helps to produce perseverance. There is an expression that is often used in the world of athletics: "No pain, no gain." Spiritually this same thing is true. Growth comes through struggle. James said that the Christian should "consider it pure joy" when he goes through various trials (James 1:2). He said that the reason to do this is because difficulties help promote growth. When Paul wrote to the church in Thessalonica he told them to "give thanks in all circumstances" (1 Thess. 5:18). Even when things are not going the way the believer would like them to go, he should give thanks anyway. That requires a great deal of faith, but it is what God desires. Stay focused on God, and allow the process to produce what He wants to produce—perseverance, character, hope, and maturity—which ultimately is the goal.

Godliness

> Godly sorrow brings repentance that leads to salvation and leaves no regret, but worldly sorrow brings death. (2 Cor. 7:10)

> Have nothing to do with godless myths and old wives' tales; rather, train yourself to be godly. For physical training is of some value, but godliness has value for all things, holding promise for both the present life and the life to come. (1 Tim. 4:7–8)

> But the day of the Lord will come like a thief. The heavens will disappear with a roar; the elements will be destroyed by fire, and the earth and everything in it will be laid bare.

> Since everything will be destroyed in this way, what kind of people ought you to be? You ought to live holy and godly lives as you look forward to the day of God and speed its coming. (2 Pet. 3:10–12a)

> His divine power has given us everything we need for life and godliness through our knowledge of him who called us by his own glory and goodness. (2 Pet. 1:3)

> For the grace of God that brings salvation has appeared to all men. It teaches us to say "No" to ungodliness and worldly passions, and to live self-controlled, upright godly lives in this present age, while we wait for the blessed hope—the glorious appearing of our great God and Savior, Jesus Christ. (Tit. 2:11–13)

These passages show us that to live a godly life means that in many ways Christians should be radically different from the world. Titus 2:11–13 tells us not only to reject ungodly and worldly passions but also to practice self-control and godliness. God has provided everything we need to live a godly life (2 Peter 1:3), but He has granted us the freedom to choose whether or not we will live that life. Christians ought to learn to be wise about good because godliness holds promise of reward, both in this life and in the one to come (1 Tim. 4:7–8).

Brotherly Kindness

Though this expression is not used anywhere else in the New Testament, the concept is certainly dealt with in many places. In the story of the Good Samaritan we see this type of kindness being expressed. We see the heart that needs to be displayed in the following verses:

Be devoted to one another in brotherly love. Honor one another above yourselves. (Rom. 12:10)

Do nothing from selfishness or empty conceit, but with humility of mind let each of you regard one another as more important than himself, do not *merely* look out for your own personal interests, but also for the interests of others. Have this attitude in yourselves which was also in Christ Jesus, who, although He existed in the form of God, did not regard equality with God a thing to be grasped, but emptied Himself, taking the form of a bond-servant, *and* being made in the likeness of men. And being found in appearance as a man, He humbled Himself by becoming obedient to the point of death, even death on a cross. (Phil. 2:3–8, NASB)

These passages tell us to look at the needs of our brothers and sisters and to help meet those needs. Do not merely look out for your own interests by for theirs as well (Phil. 2:4). Honor your brother (Rom. 12:10) and serve him (Phil. 2:3–8).

Love

> By this all men will know that you are my disciples, if you love one another. (John 13:35)

Love is the real test of our relationship with God. It is because of love that we choose to obey our Lord (John 14:15). If we love, the world will know that we follow Christ (John 13:35). Listen to the words of John in the following passage:

> Dear friends, let us love one another, for love comes from God. Everyone who loves has been born of God and knows God. Whoever does not love does not know God because God is love. This is how God showed his love among us: He sent his one and only Son into the world that we might live through him. This is love: not that we loved God, but that he loved us and sent his Son as an atoning sacrifice for our sins. Dear friends, since God so loved us, we also ought to love one another. No one has ever seen God; but if we love one another, God lives in us and his love is made complete in us." (1 John 4:7–12)

God's people must dedicate themselves to love—love for God and love for one another.

In 2 Peter 1:5–11, we're given a wonderful formula for success in the spiritual arena. It could be written like this: Faith + Moral Excellence + Knowledge + Self-control + Perseverance + Brotherly Kindness + Love = You Will Never Stumble and You Will Receive An Abundant Entrance Into Heaven.

The disciple of Christ would be wise to follow the "blueprint" that God left for us in this passage.

Food for thought:

- As you study the concepts presented today, ask the Lord to show you which of these areas you need to grow in.
- Commit to doing all that you can to grow in each area listed in 2 Peter 1. We are promised that if we are growing in each of the areas listed, we will never stumble.
- Study, pray, and apply. Allow the Lord to mold you into the strong, vibrant believer He desires for you to be.

Day Thirty-nine

Gaining the Victory

The God of peace will soon crush Satan under your feet. (Rom. 16:20)

As we have looked at the concept of learning to be wise about what is good and innocent about what is evil, we have spent a great deal of time looking at what *we* are responsible for. Yes, we have looked at the role of the Spirit and the impossibility of being able to live a godly life without His work, but most of what we have discussed has been focused on what we need to do in response to what God has provided for us to be able to grow spiritually. As we take advantage of the things He has given, sometimes it may be easy to start thinking too highly of ourselves and our part in the maturity process. Don't! (Yes, I know that's a lot easier to say than to do.)

Immediately after Paul admonished the church in Rome to learn to be wise about what is good and innocent about what is evil he followed those words with this beautiful promise: "The God of peace will soon crush Satan under your feet" (Rom. 16:20).

As we examine this text, we will look at a couple of very important truths. First, God is the one who will do the "crushing." Second, He will soon crush Satan "under your feet."

"The God of peace . . ." God is the one who brings peace. Christ is called the Prince of Peace (Isa. 9:6). He is the one who provides the "peace that passes understanding" (Phil. 4:7). As you go through life, remember that God is not the author of turmoil or of suffering. He is not the one who makes us choose things that are destructive. No, He is the God of peace. He wants you to be free. He is the one who has given us "*everything*" we need for life and godliness" (2 Peter 1:3, emphasis added).

". . . will soon crush Satan under your feet." God promises you victory. Often people start looking at Satan's power and thinking that there is no hope of resisting him. But James 4:7 tells us that if we resist him he will flee. 1 Peter 5:9 tells us to resist him and to stand firm in the faith. In Ephesians 6, when Paul talked about putting on the "full armor," he said that if we take up the shield of faith we can "extinguish all the flaming arrows of the evil one" (vs. 16).

Food for thought:

- What changes in your perspective when you realize that God is the one who is soon going to crush Satan?
- How should your life change by staying in closer fellowship with the God of peace?
- Does knowing that God will soon crush Satan under your feet change how you should react when you come under attack?

Day Forty

Tying It All Together

> I want you to be wise about what is good, and innocent about what is evil. (Rom. 16:19)

This entire study has been focused on learning what this verse means and how the Christian can put it into practice in his daily life. Brooks and Winbery stated it like this: "I want you to be experts *about good* but simpletons *about evil*."[57]

We are God's children and know that when Christ appears we are going to see Him as He is and we'll be made like Him. Everyone who has that hope will purify himself (1 John 3:2–3). Since we are going to be made like Christ when He returns, our lives now should be focused on being pure just as He is pure. A wonderful place to begin would be by keeping our eyes focused on Jesus, the author and the perfector of our faith (Heb. 12:2–3). It is also important to remember that as God's children our citizenship is now a heavenly one (Phil. 3:20). We must not allow ourselves to live the same way the world does, because we are no longer "of the world," even though for the time being we do continue to live in it. As Christians we are now a "new creation" (2 Cor. 5:17). We have been called out of darkness and into God's marvelous light (1 Peter 2:9–10).

What are some of the things that we can do to be wise about good and innocent about evil? We can begin by doing what Paul told the church in Rome in Romans 12:2: "Do not conform any longer to the pattern of this world, but be transformed by the renewing of your mind." Some of the things we can do to help in this process would include changing the things that we look at (Luke 11:34; Job 31:1; Matt. 5:28–30); dwelling on those things that are true, noble, right, pure, lovely, admirable, excellent, or praiseworthy (Phil. 4:8); sowing to the Spirit rather than to the flesh (Gal. 6:8); and practicing the "replacement principle." (Any time we get rid of sin in our lives, we must replace it with godly behavior.)

We must allow the Spirit to lead us in our lives, because it is the ones who are led by the Spirit of God who are sons of God (Rom. 8:14). The Spirit helps us to put to death the deeds of the flesh (Rom. 8:13). If we sow to the Spirit rather than to the flesh, we will reap eternal life (Gal. 6:7–10).

There are a lot of different spiritual tools that we can utilize in order to grow wiser about those things that are good (Rom. 16:19). Some of them are studying, meditating, praying, examining ourselves, memorizing Scripture, fasting, praising, serving others, forgiving, associating with godly people, and loving. Another important thing to always keep in mind is to make sure that we always have on the full armor of God (Eph. 6:10–18).

Yesterday we saw a "blueprint" for success (2 Pet. 1:5–11). God has given us everything that we need for godliness (which is truly being wise about good). We are told that everyone who has the hope of being like Jesus when he returns will purify himself (1 John 3:2–3).

Ultimately, being wise about good means that we are growing in our knowledge of God (2 Pet. 1:3) and are growing more and more like Christ. This is not merely intellectual knowledge, but it is faith put into action (James 1:22; 2:14–26).

Learning to take each thought captive and make it obedient to Christ (2 Cor. 10:5) will help us to return to innocence about evil. Though this is impossible for man on his own, it is good to know that we serve a God with whom all things are possible (Matt. 19:26; Mark 19:27; Luke 18:27).

"Since we have these promises, dear friends, let us purify ourselves from everything that contaminates body and spirit, perfecting holiness out of reverence for God" (2 Cor. 7:1).

Please make the commitment that you will do as James said in James 1:22 "Do not merely listen to the word, and so deceive yourselves, Do what it says."

It is my hope and prayer that you will take the truths we have discussed and that you will commit to cultivating purity of heart.

Food for thought:

- We have covered a lot of territory. I hope you will spend a great deal of time studying, praying, and applying what you've learned and that you will do all that you need to do to grow closer to the Lord.
- Strive to become a person of prayer and a person through whom God will constantly be glorified.
- Realize that God has given you everything that you need for life and for godliness (2 Peter 1:3). But also realize that even though He has provided the way to maturity or to "innocence" for you, He expects you to take advantage of all that He has provided.

Dear Lord,

It is my hope and prayer that all those who read this material will be richly blessed and that You will help them to learn to be wise about those things that are good and to return to being innocent about all that is evil. Let Your name be glorified in their lives.

In Jesus Holy Name, Amen!

BIBLIOGRAPHY

Alcoholics Anonymous. *Alcoholics Anonymous.* New York, NY: Alcoholics Anonymous World Services, Inc., 1976.

Anderson, Lynn. *If I Really Believe, Why Do I Have These Doubts?* Minneapolis, MN: Bethany House Publishers, 1992.

Andrew, Brother. *God's Smuggler.* Uhrichsville, OH: Barbour and Company, 1967.

Arthur, Kay. *A Call to Follow Jesus.* Eugene, OR: Harvest House Publishers, 1994.

Arthur, Kay. *Desiring God's Own Heart.* Eugene, OR: Harvest House Publishers, 1997.

Arthur, Kay. *Free From Bondage God's Way.* Eugene, OR: Harvest House Publishers, 1994.

Ogilvie, Lloyd J., ed. *The Communicator's Commentary, Romans.* Waco, TX: Word Books, Publisher, 1982.

Barnes, Albert. *Notes on the New Testament.,* Grand Rapids, MI: Baker Book House, 1959.

Bauer, Walter. *A Greek-English Lexicon of the New Testament and Other Early Christian Literature,* 2nd ed. Revised by William F. Arndt, F. Wilbur Gingrich and Frederick W. Danker. Chicago, IL: University of Chicago Press, 1979.

Blackaby, Henry T. and Claude V. King. *Experiencing God.* Nashville, TN: Broadman & Holman Publishers, 1994.

Boles, H. Leo. *New Testament Commentaries, Romans.* Nashville, TN: Gospel Advocate Company, 1989.

Bright, Bill. *A Handbook for Christian Maturity.* San Bernardino, CA: Here's Life Publishers, Inc., 1982.

Bright, Bill, Edwin Cole, Dr. James Dobson, Tony Evans, Bill McCartney, Luis Palau, Randy Phillips, Gary Smalley, *Seven Promises of a Promise Keeper,* Colorado Springs, CO: Focus on the Family, 1994.

Brooks, James A. and Carlton L. Winberg. *Syntax of New Testament Greek.* Washington, DC: University Press of America, 1979.

Bromiley, Geoffrey W. *Theological Dictionary of the New Testament.* Grand Rapids, MI: William B. Eerdmans Publishing Company, 1985.

Bryan, Alan. *Climb Happiness Hill.* Nashville, TN: Christian Development Institute, 1978.

Bibliography

Bullinger, Ethelbert W. *A Critical Lexicon and Concordance to the English and Greek New Testament.* Grand Rapids, MI: Zondervan Publishing House, 1975.

Burke, Dennis. *Yielding to the Holy Spirit.* Tulsa, OK: Harrison House, Inc., 1993.

Burrows, W. *The Preacher's Homiletic Commentary.* Grand Rapids, MI: Baker Book House, 1996.

Carothers, Merlin R. *Power in Praise.* Plainfield, NJ: Logos, International, 1972.

Caton, David E. *Overcoming the Addiction to Pornography.* Lake Mary, FL: Accord Books, 1990.

Reimann, James, ed. *My Utmost for His Highest.* Grand Rapids, MI: Discovery House Publishers, 1992.

Clarke, Adam. *New Testament Commentary,* New York, NY: T. Mason and G. Lane, 1837.

Coffman, James Burton. *Commentary on the Gospel of Matthew.* Austin, TX: Firm Foundation Publishing House, 1968.

Davies, Peter, ed. *The American Heritage Dictionary of the English Language.* New York, NY: Harper & Row, Publishers, 1923.

Deere, Jack. *Surprised by the Power of the Spirit.* Grand Rapids, MI: Zondervan Publishing House, 1993.

Douglas, J. D., ed. *The New Bible Dictionary.* Grand Rapids, MI: William B. Eerdmans Publishing Co., 1962.

Eims, LeRoy. *What Every Christian Should Know About Growing*, 3rd ed. Wheaton, IL: Victor Books, 1977.

Exell, Joseph S., ed. *The Biblical Illustrator*, Twenty-three Volume Edition. Grand Rapids, MI: Baker Book House, 1982. First published by Rebell from 1890 to 1900.

Floyd, Ronnie W. *The Power of Prayer and Fasting.* Nashville, TN: Broadman & Holman Publishers, 1997.

Friberg, Barbara and Timothy Friberg, eds. *Analytical Greek New Testament.* Grand Rapids, MI: Baker Book House, 1981.

Gilbrant, Thoralf and Tor Inge Gilbrant. *The New Testament Greek-English Dictionary.* Springfield, MS: The Complete Biblical Library, 1986, Vol. Zeta-Kappa.

Gill, A. L. *God's Promises for Your Every Need.* Dallas, TX: Word Publishing, 1995.

Harris, R. Laird, ed. *Theological Wordbook of the Old Testament.* Chicago, IL: Moody Press, 1980.

Hook, Cecil. *Free in Christ.* New Braunfels, TX: Self-Published, 1985.

The Holy Bible, King James Version. Iowa Falls, IA: Riverside Book & Bible House, 1996.

The Holy Bible, New American Standard Bible. Cambridge, England: Cambridge University Press, 1977.

Bibliography

The Holy Bible, New International Version. Grand Rapids, MI: Zondervan Publishing House, 1994.

The Holy Bible, Revised Standard Version. Nelson, Nashville, TN: Thomas Nelson Inc., 1972.

Howard, Alton H., ed. *Songs of the Church, 21st Century Edition.* West Monroe, LA: Howard Publishing Co., Inc., 1994.

Jeremiah, David. *Prayer the Great Adventure.* Sisters, OR: Multnomah Publishers, Inc., 1997.

Johnston, J. Kirk. *Why Christians Sin.* Grand Rapids, MI: Discovery House Publishers, 1992.

Keil, C. F. and F. Delitzsch. *Commentary on the Old Testament.* Peabody, MA: Hendrickson Publishers, 1966, Vol. 6.

Kempis, Thomas à. *Imitation of Christ.* New York, NY: Grosset & Dunlap, 1972.

LaHaye, Tim. *Transforming Your Temperament.* New York, NY: Inspiration Press, 1991.

Lawson, LeRoy. *Come to the Party, Celebrate Jesus.* Cincinnati, OH: Standard Publishing Company, 1994.

Lewis, David K., Carley H. Dodd, Darryl L. Tippens *The Gospel According to Generation X,* Abilene, TX: A.C.U. Press, 1995.

Littauer, Florence. *Personality Plus,* Grand Rapids, MI: Fleming H. Revell, 1997.

Littauer, Fred and Florence Littauer. *Freeing Your Mind from Memories that Bind.* San Bernardino, CA: Here's Life Publishers, Inc., 1990.

Lloyd-Jones, D. Martyn. *Studies in the Sermon on the Mount.* Grand Rapids, MI: William B. Eerdmans Publishing Company, 1974.

Lucado, Max. *On the Anvil.* Wheaton, IL: Tyndale House Publishers, 1985.

Lucado, Max. *Just Like Jesus.* Nashville, TN: Word Publishing, 1998.

Martin, Glen S. and Dian Ginter. *Drawing Closer.* Nashville, TN: Broadman & Holman Publishers, 1995.

McDowell, Josh. *Right From Wrong.* Dallas, TX: Word Publishing, 1994.

McLaughlin, Don. *Heaven in the Real World.* West Monroe, LA: Howard Publishing Co., 1997.

Moulton, Harold K. *The Analytical Greek Lexicon Revised.* Grand Rapids, MI: Zondervan Publishing House, 1978.

Murray, Andrew. *The Power of the Blood of Jesus,* Springdale, PA: Whitaker House, 1993.

Murray, Andrew. *With Christ in the School of Prayer.* Chicago, IL: M. A. Donohue & Co., 1885.

Murray, Andrew. *The Believer's Absolute Surrender.* Minneapolis, MN: Bethany House 1985.

Bibliography

Nee, Watchman. *Changed into His Likeness.* Wheaton, IL: Tyndale House Publishers, Inc., 1980.

Nee, Watchman. *Sit, Walk, Stand.* Wheaton, IL: Tyndale House Publishers, Inc. 1977.

Nee, Watchman. *The Normal Christian Life.* Wheaton, IL: Tyndale House Publishers, Inc., 1981.

Ogilvie, Lloyd John. *Discovering God's Will in Your Life.* Eugene, OR: Harvest House Publishing, 1982.

Peterson, Lorraine. *If God Loves Me, Why Can't I Get My Locker Open?* Minneapolis, MN: Bethany House Publishers, 1983.

Rainer, Thom S. *The Bridger Generation.* Nashville, TN: Broadman & Holman Publishers, 1997.

Rienicker, Fritz and Cleon Rogers. *Linguistic Key to the Greek New Testament.* Grand Rapids, MI: Regency Reference Library, 1980.

Ryrie, Charles Caldwell, ed. *Ryrie Study Bible Expanded Edition, New American Standard Bible.* Chicago, IL: Moody Press, 1995.

Sheldon, Charles. *In His Steps.* Old Tappan, NJ: Fleming R. Revell Company, 1979.

Spurgeon, C.H. *The Gospel of the Kingdom.* London: Fleming H. Revell Company, 1913.

Stanley, Charles. *How to Listen to God.* Richmond, BC: Thomas Nelson, Inc., Publishers, 1985.

Stanley, Charles. *The Glorious Journey.* Nashville, TN: Thomas Nelson Publishers, 1996.

Strong, James. *The Exhaustive Concordance of the Bible.* Peabody, MA, Hendrickson Publishers, first published in 1894.

Stuart, Moss. *Commentary on the Epistle to the Romans.* New York, NY: Gould and Newman, 1835.

Sumrall, Lester. *Overcoming Compulsive Desires.* Springdale, PA: Whitaker House, 1990.

Swindoll, Charles. *Flying Closer to the Flame.* Dallas, TX: Word Publishing, 1993.

Swindoll, Charles R. *Three Steps Forward Two Steps Back.* Nashville, TN: Thomas Nelson Publishers, 1980.

Swindoll, Charles R. *The Quest for Character.* Grand Rapids, MI: Zondervan Publishing House, 1982.

Taylor, Jack. *Hallelujah Factor.* Nashville, TN: Broadman Press, 1983.

Verlag, W. Kohlhammer. *Theological Dictionary of the New Testament,* Trans. Geoffrey W. Bromiley. Grand Rapids, MI: William B. Eerdmans Publishing Company, 1985.

Wescott, Brooke Foss, and Fenton John Anthony Hort. *The New Testament in the Original Greek.* New York, NY: The MacMillan Company, 1943.

White, Edwin F. *A Sense of Presence.* Nashville, TN: Christian Communications, 1989.

Wilkes, Peter. *Winning the War Within.* Downers Grove, IL: Intervarsity Press, 1995.

Wilson, William. *New Wilson's Old Testament Word Studies.* Grand Rapids, MI: Kregel Publications, 1987.

Zodhiates, Spiros. *The Complete Word Study Dictionary New Testament.* Iowa Falls, IA: Word Bible Publishers, Inc., 1992.

ENDNOTES

[1] Josh McDowell, *Right From Wrong* (Dallas, TX: Word Publishing, 1994) p. 6. Compiled from figures published by the Children's Defense Fund and the book, *13th Generation*, by Neil Howe and Bill Strauss, p. 33

[2] Ibid., pp. 14–15. Survey done by the Barna Research Group. More than 3,700 young people were surveyed. They used a scientifically designed process and randomly selected youth from thousands of churches throughout the U.S. and Canada, p. 8.

[3] D. Martyn Lloyd-Jones, *Studies in the Sermon on the Mount* (Grand Rapids, MI: Wm. B. Eerdmans Publishing Company, 1974), p. 43.

[4] Henry T. Blackaby and Claude V. King, *Experiencing God* (Nashville, TN: Broadman & Holman Publishers, 1994), p. 32.

[5] C.F. Keil and F. Delitzsch, *Commentary on the Old Testament, Volume 6, Proverbs, Ecclesiastes, Song of Solomon* (Peabody, MA: Hendrickson Publishers, 1966), p. 218.

[6] J. D. Douglas, ed. *The New Bible Dictionary* (Grand Rapids, MI: William B. Eerdmans Publishing Co., 1962), pp. 481–482.

[7] McDowell, *Right From Wrong*, p. 97

[8] William Wilson, *New Wilson's Old Testament Word Studies* (Grand Rapids, MI: Kregel Publications, 1987), p. 230.

[9] Compare to 2 Kings 24:2–4.

[10] Please note that the command is to hate sin, not to hate the person who commits that sin. If we were to hate the sinner we would have to hate everyone, because we have all sinned (Rom. 3:23).

[11] Please note that I am not saying that we will become sinless people. John said in 1 John 1:10 that if we claim to be without sin we are liars. The beauty of the new life in Christ is that we have been set free and are a forgiven people.

[12] Bill Bright, et al, *Seven Promises of a Promise Keeper*, (Colorado Springs, CO: Here's Life Publishers, Inc., 1994), pp. 85–89.
[13] Ibid., pp. 76–79.
[14] Wm. J. Kirkpatrick, "O To Be Like Thee," Songs *of the Church, Twenty-First Century Edition*, Alton H. Howard, ed. (West Monroe, LA: Howard Publishing Co., 1994), p. 358.
[15] Don McLaughlin, *Heaven in the Real World* (West Monroe, LA: Howard Publishing Co., 1997), p. 39.
[16] Charles Sheldon, , *In His Steps*. (Old Tappan, NJ: Fleming R. Revell Company, 1979), p. 16.
[17] Lucado, *Just Like Jesus*, p. 1.
[18] LeRoy Eims, *What Every Christian Should Know About Growing* (Wheaton, IL: Victor Books, 1977), p. 131.
[19] Thomas à Kempis, *Imitation of Christ* (New York, NY: Grosset & Dunlap, 1972), p. 1.
[20] Albert E. Brumley, Arr., *Songs of the Church, Twenty-First Century Edition,* Alton H. Howard, ed. (West Monroe, LA: Howard Publishing Co., 1994), p. 496.
[21] Peter Wilkes, *Winning the War Within* (Dowers Grove, IL: Intervarsity Press, 1995), p. 71.
[22] Ibid., p. 45.
[23] Andrew Murray, *The Believer's Absolute Surrender* (Minneapolis, MN: Bethany House 1985), pp. 31–41.
[24] Quoted in Charles Stanley, *How to Listen to God* (Richmond, BC: Thomas Nelson, 1985), p. 111.
[25] Ibid., pp. 112–120.
[26] Lester Sumrall, *Overcoming Compulsive Desires* (Springdale, PA: Whitaker House, 1990), p. 56.
[27] Charles Stanley, *The Glorious Journey* (Nashville, TN: Thomas Nelson Publishers, 1996), pp. 130–131.
[28] Murray, *The Believer's Absolute Surrender*, p. 76.
[29] Hannah Whitall Smith, *The Christian's Secret of a Happy Life,* (Old Tappan, NJ: Revell, 1968), quoted in J. Kirk Johnston, *Why Christians Sin* (Grand Rapids, MI: Discovery House Publishers, 1992), p. 176.
[30] Ronnie W. Floyd, *The Power of Prayer and Fasting* (Nashville, TN: Broadman & Holman Publishers, 1997), p. 125.
[31] Peter Wilkes, *Winning the War Within* (Madison, WI: Intervarsity Press, 1995), pp. 15–16
[32] Ibid, p. 17.
[33] Ibid., p. 45.
[34] Lester Sumrall, *Overcoming Compulsive Desires*, p. 62.
[35] Letzer, Erwin, quoted in Ibid., pp. 48–49.
[36] Ibid., p. 52.
[37] Al-Anon, Emotions Anonymous, Fear of Success Anonymous, Sexual Assault Recovery Anonymous, Sex and Love Addicts Anonymous, Nicotine Anonymous, Ho-

Endnotes

mosexual Anonymous, Phobics Anonymous and Depressives Anonymous, just to name a few.

[38] Author Unstated, *Alcoholics Anonymous,* (New York, NY: Alcoholics Anonymous World Services, 1976), pp. 59–60.

[39] Sumrall, *Overcoming Compulsive Desires*, p. 97.

[40] Ibid., p. 98.

[41] Ibid., p. 70.

[42] Ibid., p. 72.

[43] Tozer, A. W., quoted in Ibid., p. 54.

[44] Ethelbert Bullinger, *A Critical Lexicon and Concordance to the English and Greek New Testament* (Grand Rapids, MI: Zondervan Publishing House, 1975), p. 638.

[45] Johnston, *Why Christians Sin,* p. 122.

[46] R. Laid Harris, ed., *Theological Wordbook of the Old Testament*, Volume 2 (Chicago, IL: Moody Press, 1980), pp. 875–876.

[47] Ibid., p. 876.

[48] Lucado, *Just Like Jesus*, p. 47–49.

[49] If the source of your struggle is your spouse, then there are other answers. God's will is for you to remain with your spouse if it is at all possible and for you to bring peace to the relationship (2 Corinthians 7).

[50] Floyd, *The Power of Prayer*, pp. 161–167.

[51] Jack R. Taylor, *The Hallelujah Factor* (Nashville, TN: Broadman Press, 1983), p. 32.

[52] Ibid., pp. 37–40.

[53] Ibid., p. 33.

[54] Sumrall, *Overcoming Compulsive Desires,* p. 34.

[55] Eims, *What Every Christian Should Know* , p. 129.

[56] Bullinger, *A Critical Lexicon*, p. 849.

[57] James A. Brooks and Carlton L. Winbery, *Syntax of New Testament Greek,* (Washington, DC: University Press of America, 1979), p. 52.

Dr. Richardson also conducts *Return to Innocence Seminars*. The seminar can be very general and deal with overcoming any type of habitual sin, or it can be geared to specific sin, depending on the audience's needs. Contact Information:

PassionforPurity@hotmail.com

To order additional copies of

Return to Innocence

Have your credit card ready and call:

1-877-421-READ (7323)

or please visit our web site at
www.pleasantword.com

Also available at:
www.amazon.com
and
www.barnesandnoble.com

CPSIA information can be obtained at www.ICGtesting.com
Printed in the USA
LVOW08s0823201013

357684LV00002B/630/A